Language in Action

An Introduction to Modern Linguistics

Joanne Kenworthy

Longman

London and New York

9388

Longman Group UK Limited,
Longman House, Burnt Mill, Harlow,
Essex CM20 2JE, England
and Associated Companies throughout the world.

© Longman Group Limited 1991

Published in the United States of America by
Longman Inc., New York

First published 1991

ISBN 0 582 03583 X

Set in Linotron 300, 10/12pt Meridien

Produced by Longman Group (FE) Ltd
Printed in Hong Kong

British Library Cataloguing
in Publication Data
Kenworthy, Joanne
Language in action : an introduction to
modern linguistics.
1. Linguistics
I. Title
410

Library of Congress Cataloging
in Publication data
  Language in action : an introduction to
  modern linguistics /
Joanne Kenworthy
    p. cm.
  ISBN 0-582-03583-X
  1. Linguistics.   I. Title.
P121.K45   1991   410--dc20   90-48619
                                        CIP

Acknowledgements
We are grateful to the following for permission to reproduce
copyright material:

Faber and Faber Ltd. for an extract from the Introduction to *The
Seventh Seal* by Ingmar Bergman, trans. Larf Malstrom & David
Kushner; the author, Dr. M. Smith for his abridged article 'Red in
tooth and claw' from *The Weekend Guardian* (25/26.3.89).

We are grateful to the following for permission to reproduce
copyright photographs:

© BBC for page 116. © by permission of the Syndics of
Cambridge University Library for page 2.   © Crown
copyright/HMSO for page 101. Charles F. Hockett for page 79.
Drawing by Ross; © 1974 The New Yorker Magazine, Inc. for
page 114. Camera Press for page 83. Punch Publications Ltd for
page 56. © 1974 United Feature Syndicate, Inc. for page 27. ©
1980 NEA, Inc./United Media for page 43. © 1981 Universal
Press Syndicate for page 25.

Contents

Introduction

The aim of this book is to present a survey of modern linguistics, the 'scientific study of language'. As with other disciplines, linguistics has various branches. In Chapter One, 'Words', we look at how linguists describe the meaning and the structure of words. In Chapter Two, 'Sounds', we examine phonetics and phonology, the branches of linguistics that deal with how sounds are produced and the way languages organise sounds to convey differences in meaning. Chapter Three, 'Sentences', describes the study of words in sequence – 'grammar' or 'syntax'. Chapter Four looks at 'Texts and Conversations' to see how linguists study the larger patterns of meaning in 'discourse'. Most of the examples used will be from English, but the overall aim is to give a picture of how linguists work, how they approach the study of any language.

When studying language, no matter how detailed and specific the analysis becomes, one must not lose sight of the fact that human language is a means of communication between people. We speak to each other face-to-face, with current technology we can now speak to each other over great distances. We use writing when speaking is impossible or inappropriate, and we can read what was written down centuries ago, and write texts for people we have never met and will never meet. Sometimes our speech is a form of social contact; sometimes we need to exchange vital pieces of information; our writing may also simply be a means of 'keeping in touch' or can be used to explain (as in this book) or to entertain, enlighten, stimulate thought, pass down traditions, etc.

The form of language is determined by its media and purposes. And because the use of language is a kind of action, each chapter in this book will contain a section which explores some aspects of sounds, words, sentences, texts, 'in action'.

Chapter One

Words

In this chapter we will be looking at how linguists study word meaning and the structure of words in language. The goal of linguists in studying language at the level of words is to be able to represent what native speakers know about words and their meanings. The phrase 'the meaning of a word' prompts most people to think in terms of dictionary definitions. But native speakers know and use words long before they learn how to use a dictionary – most children say their first word around the age of one year. We shall take as our starting point what young children know about words and meaning. The following two short conversations took place in a primary school classroom. Let us examine what these children know about words in English.[1]

Teacher to small group of primary school children (aged 6 and 7):

Teacher: What is a word?
Shirley: It . . . it's a bit of language.
Pritti: It . . . when you talk . . . like when you say 'blue'.
Teacher: That's very good.
Wayne: When you think hard . . . you get the sense in your head.

A few minutes later the following conversation took place – the teacher had asked the children to try to make up as many words as they could from the letters in the word *orchestra* (they have already discovered such possibilities as *chest, roar* and *are,* etc.).

James: I've got nine words!
Teacher: Who can find another one?
James: I've got it! c–r–e–t.
Teacher: 'Cret'! 'Cret' isn't a word.
James: Well . . . no . . . but I could make it mean something.
Teacher: Could you? Then would it be a word?
James: Well . . . if I told everybody what it meant . . . yes.

These young schoolchildren are aware of some central points about words in language – that words are symbols which have meanings, or, as

Wayne puts it, 'a sense', and that these meanings are shared by speakers of a particular language. James knows that he could think up a meaning for c–r–e–t, but if he didn't tell everyone then it would not count as a word in the English language. The linguist, de Saussure, used the phrase 'linguistic sign'[2] to describe a 'word'.

Ferdinand de Saussure (1857–1913) His book, A Course in Modern Linguistics, *is widely considered to be the foundation of the modern subject of linguistics.*

Words have meanings, and as speakers of a language we assume that when we use a word our listeners attach the same meaning to it, and therefore understand what we are talking about. Of course, they may not know a word or words we use at all, and then we get involved in giving explanations or definitions. Let us consider what is involved in defining a word.

Defining words

By far the simplest, most straightforward cases of giving definitions are those words which are names of objects of which there is only *one* – *proper names*, e.g. Westminster Abbey or the Leaning Tower of Pisa or Mount Fuji. As proper names these words have *direct reference*. They denote a specific object, person, place, etc., in the world. These proper names are also a good demonstration that the word or name is an arbitrary sign. There is no link or resemblance between the word and the object it denotes. An object, person or place doesn't change its nature by having its name changed. Juliet knew her Romeo would be the same person if he were called by a different name, ('A rose by any other name would smell as sweet') and when St Petersburg in Russia was renamed Petrograd, and then Leningrad, nothing about the city changed physically.

Sometimes words *have* been chosen as the name for something because of a sound resemblance, although this is relatively rare in all languages. These are called *phonaesthetic* words – the name imitates the thing. Young children's early words are often representations of the sounds that objects make: *woof-woof* is used by English-speaking children for *dog*, and *meow* for *cat*. Every language probably has some of these phonaesthetic words (some examples from English are *buzz, twitter, cheep, chug, hiss*, etc.) but although they are interesting cases, and perhaps give us an insight into the origins of human language, they are still in the minority. Most words are arbitrary symbols or signs.

The task of giving the meaning of proper names – words that have direct reference – is fairly simple; they mean the specific object, place, institution, person, etc. that they refer to, i.e. they have direct and unique reference. Suppose James had decided that he wanted his new word 'cret' to mean the small pond at the end of the garden behind his house. All that James would need to do to 'tell everybody what it meant' would be to show them the pond and say 'This is called the Cret'. He would be using one type of definition – *ostensive definition*, literally 'definition by pointing'.

However, what if James wanted the word 'cret' to mean 'the area of floor directly beneath any piece of furniture'? He could not really use ostensive definition because rather than referring to a unique object or person, the word 'cret' would be used to refer to a class of things, as *window, cup, lamp, room*, etc., do. Each 'cret' would be slightly different from any other, just as each cup or room is slightly different from any other. These words are termed *common nouns* by linguists (as opposed to proper names/nouns). So ostensive definition is of limited value in defining common nouns – our understanding of the word 'cret' would depend on our ability to recognise the shared properties of each example of a 'cret' that we were shown or came across. It is also important to remember a basic difficulty in defining words with other words – if James simply gave people a verbal definition using the words in quotations above, then the listeners' understanding would depend on their prior understanding of the words in the definition itself, e.g. *area, furniture, beneath*. Defining a common noun can be very frustrating if your listener doesn't know the meaning of the words you use in your definition.

The problems of definition would be increased if James decided that he

3

wanted to use the word 'cret' as a symbol for an abstract idea (an *abstract noun*) or an action (a *verb*). Suppose James wanted 'cret' to be a verb meaning 'the way you eat food that you don't like but must eat because your parents say it is good for you'. In this situation James could use a different kind of definition – he could find words that were related in meaning, such as *gobble, eat, consume*, etc. These words share some elements of meaning and he could use them to help specify the meaning of 'cret'. (Of course, as mentioned above, he would still need to assume that his listeners already knew and understood the meaning of the related words, *eat, gobble*, etc.)

But James could possibly give his listeners a clearer idea of what it meant to 'cret' by providing some examples of the word used in sentences; for example, 'Yesterday it took me half an hour to cret my vegetables at dinner – I hate vegetables' or 'Fortunately for her, my little sister didn't need to cret her soup because Grandmother was visiting'. The words that co-occur with 'cret' could give some indication of its meaning. In the above sentences they would show that 'cretting' was not a pleasant task. Even more information about the meaning of the word could be supplied by specifying what restrictions there are on its use. Some words may only be used in very formal contexts, some words may be restricted to scientific or technical uses, and so on. James could explain that 'to cret' was an informal expression, like *to mess about, to have a go, to wallop*, etc.

What is clear from this brief discussion is that the description of the meaning of a word is by no means a simple task. On the contrary, it is a very complex task which involves a number of *perspectives*:

1) the referential relation between the word and an entity in the world – in linguistics this is termed its *denotation*.
2) the relation between the word and other words in the language – its *sense relations*.
3) the other words which co-occur with it in the language – the technical term used is its *collocations*.
4) the use of the word in the language in terms of restrictions – its *communicative value*.

This list of perspectives constitutes the area of study in modern linguistics known as *lexical semantics*. In linguistics, word meaning is studied by detailed analysis of the way words are used. Its primary focus is 'the way people relate words to each other within the framework of their language'.[3] This emphasis is reflected in the statement by the linguistic philosopher, Ludwig Wittgenstein (1889–1951) – 'the meaning of a word is its use in the language'. In the following sections we will examine each of the above perspectives on word meaning in more detail.

Perspectives on meaning

In Jonathan Swift's political satire *Gulliver's Travels* (1726), Gulliver visits the School of Languages in the imaginary country of Laputa. There he observes a discussion among the professors about how to improve the language of Laputa. The professors have a theory that talking is harmful: '. . . it is plain that every word we speak is in some degree a diminution of our lungs by corrosion, and consequently contributes to the shortening of our lives.'[4] To prevent this, the professors propose a plan for abolishing all words. They propose that

> . . . since words are only names for *things*, it would be more convenient for all men to carry about them such things as are necessary to express the particular business they are to discourse on . . . for short conversations a man may carry implements in his pockets or under his arms . . . But if his business be very great, and of various kinds, a man must . . . carry a great bundle of things upon his back . . ..

The professors' proposal is obviously unworkable, but it does highlight the inadequacy of the notion of *meaning* as *reference* to something in the world. Imagine you were a Laputan and you wanted to tell your friend 'My cassette recorder is broken'. You would have to put your cassette recorder in your sack and go to your friend and show him the broken recorder. But how could you make sure he knew it belonged to you? You couldn't pull *my* out of your sack – there is no object to which *my* refers, but it does have meaning – it shows the relationship between the speaker and some object or entity. And what about *broken*? You would probably have to demonstrate this using gesture. If you then wanted to say 'Please mend my cassette recorder quickly' the action of *to mend* would be an even greater challenge, and how could you show the abstract meaning of *quickly*? Rather than improving the life span of Laputans, the abolition of words would lead to total exhaustion and frustration.

As this comical example shows, the notion of words referring to something in the world is inadequate as a theory of meaning with the exception of proper names. The majority of words do not simply refer to 'things' in the world. One proposal that attempts to solve this problem is to say that words refer to *concepts* – there is an indirect relationship of reference. A version of this theory uses a *semiotic triangle* to represent this indirect reference.[5]

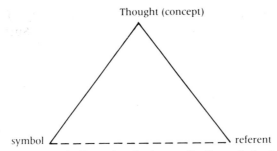

Fig. 1.1 *A semiotic triangle illustrating the theory of indirect relationship of reference*

This idea does seem satisfying in some ways – we can accept that people have an idea or concept of *love, kindness, memory* or *quickly* and that these words refer to those mental concepts. But there are still problems with words like *although, however, if,* etc. More critically, introducing the notion of mental concept doesn't get us any closer to an understanding of *what* is shared by speakers of the same language about the meaning of a word that makes communication – the exchange of meaning – possible. A botanist and a florist probably have quite different mental concepts of the word *flower*, but they both know that *The flower chewed the gum* is a strange sentence. Furthermore, any speaker of English will react to this sentence in the same way. What do the speakers of a language share about the word *flower*?

Componential analysis

One way in which linguists approach the problem of *shared meaning* is to use the technique of *componential analysis*. This involves trying to break down the meaning of words into components or units of meaning. For example, if we say *school* means *a place for study* then the word has been shown to have two components of meaning – *place* and *purpose is study*. Similarly, *hospital* could be broken down into *place* and *purpose – medical treatment. Pen* could be broken down into three components: *instrument; purpose – writing ; uses or contains ink. Pencil* would also have the first and second components, but the third would be *uses or contains graphite*.

The technique of componential analysis involves several steps. The first step is to select a group of words which seem to be connected in meaning, the assumption being that words which are connected will probably share components. This is certainly true of the examples given above – *pen* and *pencil* are connected in meaning and they share two components; *school* and *hospital* share one component. One of the first groups of words to be investigated using componential analysis was the group of words for family relationships: *mother, father, sister, brother, son,* etc. Such groups of interrelated words are termed *lexical fields* or *semantic domains.* Here are some examples:

ROOMS

room   chamber   living-room   bedroom   library   study   lounge office   kitchen   lobby   hall   foyer etc.

GEOMETRIC FIGURES

octagon   hexagon   rectangle   triangle   square   pentagon etc.

BEGINNING

start   origin   dawn   birth   conception   debut   kick-off inaugurate   introduce   beginning   inception   initiate etc.

FOLLOWING

follow   trail   pursue   shadow   tail   tag along   tread on the heels of etc.

CUPS

chalice   beaker   glass   goblet   teacup   coffee cup   wineglass tumbler etc.

CONTAINERS

vessel   bag   sack   pocket   basket   can   bucket   cask   pot bottle   basin   cup etc.

VEHICLES

train   car   bicycle   sled   motorcycle   bus   wagon etc.

Lexical fields – some questions

How many lexical fields are there? How many members does each field have? How does one decide where one lexical field ends and another begins? In the examples above, the word *cup* is a member of the field CONTAINERS but also a member of the smaller field of CUPS. There is no general agreement on these points and individual analysts are faced with difficult decisions. The decisions each analyst makes are often arbitrary. But the setting up of a lexical field is not the main concern of linguists. Their main concern is to study the *relationship* between the items in each field. If it is indeed impossible to make exact and final decisions about the number and composition of the lexical fields in a particular language (and it looks as if it is impossible) then this fact reveals something interesting about human language itself: overlap and 'fuzziness' are part of its nature.

Notice that the members of a lexical field are not restricted to single words; there are examples such as *coffee cup* and *tag along* as well as *goblet* and *pursue.* Because of the way in which English and many other languages are organised, we have to consider multi-word combinations to be single items. Linguists use the term *lexical item* to avoid confusion. So *tag along* is a lexical item made up of two words, and even though *tread on the heels of* is made up of five words, it is still considered to be a single lexical item. The term *lexical item* roughly corresponds to the form at the beginning of a dictionary entry.

Having selected a particular lexical field or semantic domain, the next step in componential analysis is to form analogies among the lexical items, and then try to identify the semantic components which emerge, based on these analogies. For example, in the lexical field of VEHICLES we can form an analogy between *car* and *motorcycle* and *wagon* and *bicycle*. A *car* is a vehicle with a motor and four wheels, a *motorcycle* has a motor and two wheels. A *wagon* has four wheels and no motor; a *bicycle* has two wheels and no motor. So, from these analogies we can identify four semantic components: VEHICLE/MOTOR/FOUR WHEELS/TWO WHEELS. (The names of components will be written in capitals to distinguish them from lexical items, e.g. *motor* versus MOTOR.) In componential analysis the symbols '+' and '−' are used as a quick and clear way to show whether a particular lexical item has a semantic component or not, for example, the item *car* does not have the component TWO WHEELS so it is '−TWO WHEELS' but '+VEHICLE, +MOTOR, and +FOUR WHEELS'. This analysis can be presented in the form of a table or grid:

	VEHICLE	MOTOR	FOUR WHEELS	TWO WHEELS
car	+	+	+	−
motorcycle	+	+	−	+
bicycle	+	−	−	+
wagon	+	−	+	−

From the above analysis it can be seen that each word shares the component VEHICLE. So this component identifies the semantic field and can be used as the name or cover term for this field. The other components have the function of distinguishing each member from every other. Notice that each word has a completely distinct set of values for the four components. Notice also that it is not necessary to use a component such as WINGS or AIR TRAVEL because this component would not distinguish any item from any other (all would be given the value 'minus'). But if *airplane, glider, helicopter*, etc. were added to our example then such a feature *would* be necessary. The aim of componential analysis is to find those components which are sufficient to describe the meaning of every lexical item in the language. In fact, the ultimate aim is to find a *universal* set of components which can be used to describe meaning in each and every language in the world.

An example of componential analysis

Let us examine a particular lexical field in detail – the field of THINGS PEOPLE WEAR or HUMAN ATTIRE. This is, of course, a fairly large field and we will restrict our discussion to eight lexical items:

belt waistband cuff collar necklace bracelet ring necktie

All of the items share the component HUMAN ATTIRE, so this can be used as the cover term for the field. The component which distinguishes *ring* and *bracelet* and *necklace* from the other items is + JEWELLERY. All the eight items share the feature GO ROUND A PART OF THE BODY – we can shorten this to +ENCIRCLE. To distinguish *necklace, bracelet* and *ring* from each other we need the components +NECK +WRIST and +FINGER. The first two components are also needed to distinguish *cuff* from *collar*, and since *belt* and *waistband* are both worn around the waist, we can propose +WAIST. With these features the grid would look like this:

	H. ATTIRE	ENCIRCLE	JEWELLERY	WAIST	WRIST	NECK	FINGER
belt	+	+	−	+	−	−	−
waistband	+	+	−	+	−	−	−
cuff	+	+	−	−	+	−	−
collar	+	+	−	−	−	+	−
necklace	+	+	+	−	−	+	−
bracelet	+	+	+	−	+	−	−
ring	+	+	+	−	−	−	+
necktie	+	+	−	−	−	+	−

Note that *belt* and *waistband* still have the same value for each component, so we need another component to distinguish them. We could use + LEATHER because belts are usually made of leather – but what about the waistband of a leather skirt? +DETACHABLE seems more satisfactory because waistbands are a part of a skirt or trousers, whereas belts are not. The component seems possible for cuff and collar (both with + value) because at one time cuffs and collars were detachable, although it doesn't seem to be particularly relevant to the modern meaning of these two lexical items. *Necktie, necklace, ring* and *bracelet* would also have to be + DETACHABLE, but again this doesn't seem to be an important part of their meanings. Maybe +DETACHABLE isn't a very useful feature and we should think of another component to distinguish *belt* from *waistband* – perhaps PART OF A GARMENT – *waistband, collar* and *cuff* are parts of skirts, shirts and trousers. Doing componential analysis certainly makes one think carefully about the meanings of words.

Some problems for componential analysis

Does componential analysis give a complete specification of the meaning of these words? Is the meaning of *necktie* – encircling piece of human attire worn around the neck? What about the fact that a necktie is usually worn by men? What about its connections with formal dress? How central are these elements of meaning to the meaning of *necktie*? This question raises an even more general question – how does one decide on centrality of meaning? If the words *crown* and *headband* had been included in the set of words, then features which are much more abstract would have to be used in order to show the symbolic meaning of *crown*, which *headband* doesn't have – in many different cultures a *crown* symbolises power, hereditary status, victory, or pre-eminence (as in sports contests). But each culture has slightly different institutions, conventions and customs, so any particular componential analysis may be 'culture-specific'. As an analytic technique it is not without problems.

The examples used so far in the discussion have all been for tangible objects; it is much more difficult to deal with abstract lexical fields. For example, consider what components would be needed to distinguish the following words for *reactions*:

disappointment anger shock rage fury confusion
amazement irritation surprise

One problem that would arise would be how to distinguish *anger, fury* and *rage*. The word *anger* does not suggest the same intensity of feeling as *rage*, and *fury* suggests even more intense feeling with possible temporary lack of control. If we propose a feature of INTENSITY then these three words could be given graded values, instead of simply + or −.

	INTENSITY
anger	1
rage	2
fury	3

As we have seen, componential analysis does have difficulties. It also has limitations – it is designed to distinguish items in a particular field from each other, and not to give a complete specification of meaning. Perhaps its most serious disadvantage is that the analysis is often *ad hoc*; there are no guidelines for deciding on either the appropriacy of features or what features are central to the meaning of a word. However, it does provide some interesting insights into word meaning. It shows us that the words of a language are organised – some words clearly 'belong together' because they are related in meaning – they 'share components'. Componential analysis has made a contribution to the study of word meaning in linguistics, but it is only one perspective on meaning. In the investigation of word meaning, linguists have also explored the *sense relations* between words.

Sense relations

Hyponymy

John Lyons has described the relationships words have with each other as a 'web of words'.[6] One relationship between words which can be studied through lexical field and componential analysis is *hyponymy*. In the analysis of the lexical field HUMAN ATTIRE we saw that the items *necklace, bracelet*, etc. shared the same feature +JEWELLERY. In lexical semantics, these words are called *hyponyms* of the word *jewellery*, and the word *jewellery* itself is called the *superordinate* term. Hyponymy is a sense relation – basically it is a relation of inclusion. The meaning of *jewellery* includes the meaning of *necklace, ring*, etc., so we can say 'A necklace is a kind of jewellery' (but not 'A jewellery is a kind of necklace'). The lexical items *necklace, ring*, etc. are co-hyponyms of *jewellery*. The relationship can be shown in a simple diagram.

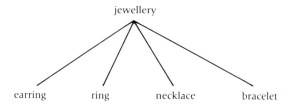

The study of the sense relation of hyponymy has revealed some very interesting differences between languages. Let us look at an example which shows how different languages can be in the way words relate to one another. Teen is a language spoken in Africa by the Tenbo people. In Teen the word *gusuko* (plant) has three co-hyponyms: *diilo* (food plants), *dansu* (plants used for making sauces) and *waro* (wild plants). These categories are very different from the lexical field of plants in English, which is based more on botanical form (*tree, fern, flower, grass, bush*, etc.) The difference between this lexical field and the lexical field of *plant* in English is demonstrated by this anecdote. A Tenbo woman was being shown the garden planted by a visiting lecturer from Europe. The lecturer asked her not to step on the flowers he had planted. She replied 'Oh, do you use these plants for your sauces?' Her remark reveals the pragmatic way she looked at 'plants' – they were wild or planted by people, edible or inedible.[7]

Native speakers are very sensitive to the relationship of hyponymy in their languages. In fact, knowing that a word is a hyponym of some superordinate term may be all that a speaker knows about a word. For example, many speakers of English know that *asp* is a kind of snake, but they know nothing else about it. Another illustration that hyponymy is

11

an important part of knowing a language is the way native speakers simplify their language when speaking to foreigners. In English, a *bonnet* is a kind of hat; it is usually worn by females as an adornment rather than as protection against bad weather and is usually decorated with ribbon and artificial flowers. When speaking to a foreigner, instead of using the word *bonnet*, a native speaker might replace it with the superordinate term *hat*, assuming that because the latter is the more inclusive word it will be easier for the foreign speaker to understand.

Incompatibility

The members of some lexical fields show the relation of incompatibility, in other words, they are *mutually exclusive*. Some good examples are the fields of geometric figures, days of the week and musical instruments. A geometric figure cannot be a triangle and a rectangle – it is one or the other. A musical instrument cannot be both a harp and a drum. But in many other fields the relation of incompatibility does not hold between items. For example, in the lexical field of *reactions* it is possible to say someone is *disappointed* and *angry* – one feeling does not exclude the other. Of course, it is only relevant to use the term 'incompatible' when discussing members of a particular lexical field – to say 'the meaning of *door* is incompatible with the meaning of *flower*' is irrelevant because *door* and *flower* do not belong to the same lexical field. But to say 'the meaning of *chair* is incompatible with the meaning of *bench*' is revealing because both are members of the lexical field of *furniture*.

Antonymy

Words may also be opposite in meaning – this is the relation of antonymy. Some common examples are:

pass – fail   dead – alive   asleep – awake
male – female   legal – illegal   boy – girl
true – false   man – woman   married – single

In the case of each of these pairs, the negative of one word implies the positive of the other – if John did not pass his examination, then he failed it; if someone is not asleep, they are awake. But the following pairs of antonyms are different:

big – small   old – young   high – low
rich – poor   good – bad   wide – narrow

If someone says 'John is not old', this does not imply 'John is young'; if Mary is not rich, then this doesn't mean she is poor. Each of these pairs represents extreme points on a scale, but there are also intermediate points. John may be middle-aged, and Mary may be 'comfortably well-off'. These antonyms are called *gradable* antonyms because degrees may be expressed. A film could be 'extremely good, quite good, fairly good, pretty bad', etc.

English speakers sometimes mix up these two types of antonyms for a special effect. For example, someone might say 'I am half–dead' to mean that they are exhausted. To be 'half-asleep' or 'half-awake' are common expressions. The sentence 'John is very married' conveys the idea that there are degrees of 'marriedness' which have very little to do with the performance of a marriage ceremony, but much more to do with certain types of behaviour, such as loyalty, fidelity, devotion, etc.

Synonymy

Synonymy is the sense relation of 'sameness of meaning'. Many speakers would consider the following pairs of words to be synonyms:

big – large   hide – conceal   astonish – amaze   receive – get
commence – begin   liberty – freedom   deep – profound

If two words have the same meaning then they should be completely interchangeable in all contexts. It is certainly true that in specific sentences one word can replace its synonym without changing the meaning of the sentence:

An elephant is a $\begin{cases} \text{big} \\ \text{large} \end{cases}$ animal.

The spy $\begin{cases} \text{hid} \\ \text{concealed} \end{cases}$ the documents.

He is always making $\begin{cases} \text{deep} \\ \text{profound} \end{cases}$ remarks at inappropriate moments.

But even if two words are interchangeable in some sentences, there may still be differences in meaning. An important question in lexical semantics is whether *strict* or *total* synonymy exists in a language or whether there is always a difference between words. Sometimes differences in meaning are a matter of style. For example, *commence* and *receive* are usually used in more formal styles than *begin* and *get*. Someone who said to his guests at an informal dinner party 'Let us commence dinner' would seem oddly over-formal. Similarly, 'We received the news yester-day' would probably be restricted to formal contexts.

An important element in meaning is the evaluative or emotional overtones a word may have. Let us take the examples *kill, murder, assassinate* and *execute*. Although all these words share the meaning *take away life*, they are clearly not total synonyms. *Murder* has elements of meaning which *kill* does not have – it implies a motive and premeditation, and most speakers think immediately of a crime of violence. *Assassinate* also implies a motive, but usually an impersonal one – many speakers think of politically motivated killing. *Execute* is used in a legal context and follows a socially sanctioned sentence of death. All these words share the basic meaning component TAKE AWAY LIFE but they each have different *connotations*.

Many words have very strong evaluative connotations. Speakers use them to show positive or negative feelings, approval or disapproval. For example, the word *fascist* is commonly applied not to members of the 'Fascist Party' but to condemn or even insult people who have particular political views or social attitudes. *Freedom-fighter* and *terrorist* have very different connotations. Generally, a speaker will refer to a group which is taking direct action in support of a cause which the speaker himself supports as *freedom-fighters*. The label *terrorist* is used to condemn actions. In reporting news events, the public media very often have extreme difficulty in finding neutral words. A word's connotations are the communicative value it has because of the feelings, images, attitudes, emotions, etc. associated with it. So, if we take connotations into account, then strict or total synonymy is probably very rare in languages.

Combinations of words

So far, we have been looking at three different perspectives on meaning: components of meaning, sense relations, and emotional or evaluative meaning – connotations. In this section we will examine combinations of words to see what effect this has on meaning. J. K. Firth (1890–1960) once said 'You shall know a word by the company it keeps'. With this statement he was drawing attention to the fact that, in any language, certain words co-occur. Linguists use the term *collocation* to refer to the 'company' a word keeps. For example, the word *broad* may occur or *collocate* with the following words:

broad
- shoulders
- river
- idea
- opinions
- daylight
- accent

In each of these combinations *broad* has a different meaning. When it collocates with words for objects, such as *shoulders* and *river*, it has a meaning of dimension close to the word *wide* i.e. 'substantial measurement from side to side or between limits'. With *idea* or *outline* it means *general* as in 'She gave me a broad idea of the plan, but now we need the details'. *Broad opinions* means *generous* opinions, which are not restricted or narrow (this meaning is close to the word *broadminded*). In the combination *broad daylight*, *broad* means 'full and clear'. *Broad accent* is a specifically British English collocation (Americans would say *strong accent*) and describes a way of speaking typical of a region as in 'He spoke with a broad Yorkshire accent' or 'She speaks broad Scots'.

Collocations are very restrictive and sometimes arbitrary. For example, *broad* can be replaced by *wide* in many combinations – it is possible to say *broad grin* and *wide grin*, or *broad river* or *wide river*. But the expression *wide shoulders* sounds slightly odd, and *wide idea*, *wide accent*, and *wide daylight* simply are 'not English'. Linguists speak of a word's *collocational restrictions*.

Some words in a language collocate very freely – think of how many words *good* can collocate with (*good questions*, *good coffee*, *good picture*, etc.). But consider *blond* and *chime* – these words are much more restricted in collocation.

The collocations of a word contribute to its meaning. This is most clearly seen in words which are restricted to only a few collocations. An example is *gnarled* – this word usually collocates with *tree* or *branch* to mean 'rough and twisted'. It can also collocate with *hands* or *fingers* and with terms for people, as in 'the gnarled old man'. *Gnash* is an even more extreme case – it only collocates with *teeth* as in 'She gnashed her teeth in rage'. If teeth are the only things that you can gnash, then this collocation must determine the meaning of the word to a very large extent.

The life of a word

In this section we will use the history of the word *enthusiasm* in English to review the notions that have been introduced in the discussion of word meaning.[8] The *Oxford English Dictionary* gives the modern sense as '. . . intensity of feeling in favour of a person, principle, cause, etc., . . . passionate eagerness in any pursuit . . .'. *Enthusiasm* first entered English in its Greek form in 1579. It had the status of a borrowed or foreign word and was always written using Greek letters. The first recorded transliteration does not occur until 1608. To those writers and scholars who knew Greek, the meaning of the word was easily derived from the meaning of its parts; in Greek *theos* has the meaning 'God' and *en* is 'in', from which the meaning 'God-in-Man' emerges. But this original meaning of supernatural possession or divine inspiration is now obsolete, and the word has undergone many changes in meaning in its 400-year history in the English language. Let us look in detail at these changes.

Early definitions

It seems that the word, with its related forms (*enthusiast, enthusiastic*), was originally a technical term restricted to the context of religion and used to describe the members of certain religious groups in ancient Greece and their behaviour. In ancient Greece there were many religious cults who worshipped particular gods and behaved as if possessed by the god (e.g. the god Bacchus) during religious rituals. In 1656, the lexicographer T. Blount in his *Glossographia* gave the following definition:

> . . . people that thought themselves inspired with a Divine spirit, and to have a clear sight of all things which they believed . . .

Two years later, in a dictionary called *The New World of Words* we have a slightly different definition: enthusiasts '. . . pretended . . . to be divinely inspired . . .' – so they could be dishonest, false, or impostors. In the 1671 edition of the dictionary there is an interesting shift of tense: 'pretended' has become 'pretend', so we know that by that date the word was being used for people living in the present as well. But 'pretend' in the eighteenth century had a wider range of meanings than it does today – it could mean 'claim' as well as its more common modern meaning of 'pose or impersonate'. The greatest lexicographer of the time, Dr Johnson, does not imply any dishonesty or 'false show' on the part of enthusiasts in his dictionary definition; he writes that these people '. . . are persuaded of some communication' with God. However, in this respect, Johnson is in conflict with another dictionary of the period. In *The New General English Dictionary* published in 1744 (11 years before Johnson's dictionary), T. Dyche and W. Pardon defined an *enthusiast* as follows:

> an enthusiast commonly means a person poisoned with the notion of being divinely inspired, when he is not, and upon that account commits a great number of irregularities in words and actions.

It seems that in the first one hundred years of its life the word *enthusiasm* had acquired negative connotations. This is clearly shown by the words used in the seventeenth- and eighteenth-century definitions, which were themselves highly evaluative:

> wild, exorbitant, false, vain, monstrous, ridiculous, inflame

These collocations in actual dictionary definitions would seem to indicate that, for some people, *enthusiasm* was a 'smear word'.

How this change of meaning came about in a word which originally referred to ancient religious cults becomes clear if we remember the religious turmoil in Britain in the seventeenth and eighteenth centuries. The Anglican Church was in conflict with the Catholic Church, on the one hand, and various Protestant groups (Presbyterians, Methodists) on the other hand. The following quotation shows how these two 'enemies' to Anglicanism were viewed:

> (Christianity suffers) '. . . by some Mens Enthusiastical Notions and Pretensions . . . .' The Church of England is 'the medium . . . between slovenly fanaticism and popish pagentry, between enthusiasm and the rational worship of God . . .'[9]

Other quotations reveal through collocations which lexical field *enthusiasm* belonged to:

> . . . gross impostors and enthusiasts . . .
> . . . infidelity, enthusiasm and bigotry . . .
> . . . credulity, enthusiasm and ignorance
> I pray God give me a clear discerning between Melancholy enthusiasm and true inspiration[10]

We could label the lexical field to which *enthusiasm* belonged as 'unorthodox, misguided religious beliefs, states of mind, or convictions'. Besides *bigotry*, *infidelity*, and *credulity* from the above quotations, other members of this lexical field would have been *fanaticism*, *zealotry* and *heresy*. In terms of degree, *enthusiasm* was probably seen as less extreme or excessive than *fanaticism* or *heresy* (so we would need graded componential features to analyse this field), but it was still viewed as a form of excess and from this it seems to have derived its negative connotations.

Extensions of meaning

Proof that the word had generally acquired negative connotations by the eighteenth century was the attempt to coin a new term which would take over the bad sense of *enthusiasm* – this was *endemoniasm*, in which the root *demon* replaced the root for god (*theo*). This was a suggestion from John Byrom, who also argued for an extension of the word in this poem written in 1757:

> What is Enthusiasm? – what can it be
> But Thought enkindled to a high degree?
> That may, Whatever be its ruling turn,
> Right or not right, with equal ardour burn?
> When to Religion we confine the word,
> What use of Language can be more absurd?[11]

Byrom's coinage was never accepted but his support for the extension of the domains of *enthusiasm* was gratified. It seems that in the eighteenth century 'to be enthusiastic' could be a good state of mind in areas *other* than religion. One writer in 1737 says that *enthusiasm* is being '. . . expelled from her religious domains . . .' and is acquiring a 'civil profession'. Another writer in 1795 points out that in religion it is a term of reproach, but that others think it neither morally good or bad:

> . . . but then they confine it to that vigour, vivacity, fervour and strength, so peculiarly manifest in the works of the Grecian, Roman, and some few of the English poets.

So, in the context of the fine arts, *enthusiasm* belonged to a very different lexical field – that of states of mind relating to creativity or literary genius. Its connotations in this domain were very positive.

It is easy to see how the term was extended to the context of literature, because the idea that poets are divinely inspired was part of the eighteenth-century literary tradition which went back to ancient Greece. In the context of literature, the word kept very different company. Here are some examples of typical collocations:

> . . . noble enthusiasm . . .
> . . . judgement, memory, understanding, enthusiasm and sensibility . . .
> . . . wild and animating enthusiasm[12]

But there are still traces of the idea of excess and even danger:

> . . . like all superlative excellencies, it (enthusiasm) verges forever on the brink of absurdity . . . (and) . . . hath some affinity to madness . . .[13]

In the context of literature, we also begin to find uses of the word referring to the reader's response, rather than the source of the writer's creativity. For example, the English were said to be 'enthusiastic' in their admiration of Shakespeare.

Further extensions of meaning

Enthusiasm was also extended to political domains in the eighteenth century. Again, we can see the source of this extension – government and religion have been closely linked in English history. Oliver Cromwell was given the label of 'enthusiast' and the French Revolution was said to prove '. . . that Enthusiasm does not belong only to religion'. In 1790 we have:

> . . . warm, eager, enthusiastic Frenchman – you deserve liberty for you know how to value it.[14]

Towards the modern meaning

All of these extensions are signs of a gradual shift in domain from the religious and quasi-religious to the secular. People could be described as responding to the beauties of nature with enthusiasm; in 1758 one writer was termed an 'enthusiast' on the subject of 'tree planting'; King George III was said to be an 'enthusiast' for Mrs Siddons, a well-known actress (today we would call him a 'fan'). There were also many protests at extensions of use. For example, in 1829 I. Taylor published a book entitled: *The Natural History of Enthusiasm* in which he protested at what he saw as the misuse of the word and tried to 'fix the term'; and another writer protested against the use of the word with reference to soldiers and scholars. However, the word continued to be extended to various contexts, many of them non-serious.

The modern meaning

In modern usage we may have railway enthusiasts, sporting enthusiasts, gossip enthusiasts, etc., and all these people demonstrate a depth of interest or admiration with no touch of disapproval. The word has lost its negative connotations completely, and now belongs to the lexical field of *mental attitudes* or *feelings*. Words such as *passion, infatuation, fascination, mania,* to be a *fan* (e.g. a football fan), to be *keen about,* or *crazy about,* to be a *crank* or *nut* (these last two have negative connotations) are other members of the field. An interesting aspect of the word's modern sense is its frequent use in job advertisements; firms advertise for a person with 'smart appearance, enthusiasm and excellent interpersonal skills,' or for someone with a 'fresh, enthusiastic approach', etc. In 400 years the word has changed from a religious technical term to a desirable – or at least positive – human characteristic.

Words in action

Meaning as style and choice

A common expression in English is 'to choose one's words carefully'. Underlying this expression is the idea that choice is meaningful – selecting a word involves rejecting others. What are some of the reasons behind the choices that speakers make? How do speakers put their store of words into action? To explore some of these issues we will examine three areas of vocabulary: euphemism, slang and jargon.

Euphemism

In English there are many ways to talk about death and dying:

to pass away   to expire   to be no more   to rest in peace
to be out of his/her misery   to go to meet his/her Maker
to cross over the Great Divide   to go to his/her final resting place

What is the difference between saying 'My father died' and 'My father passed away'? One cannot answer this question without referring to the attitude towards death in most English-speaking cultures – it is a difficult, painful topic. People's attitudes to the subject of death are reflected in their linguistic behaviour: expressions are devised which are indirect and have positive connotations – *euphemistic* expressions. The references to departure, rest, absence and travel to another world (i.e. Heaven) in the above expressions all 'soften' the taboo subject of death. The word *euphemism* is taken from Greek and means 'sound good' or 'good speech'. Euphemism is a linguistic device which recognises the conventions and attitudes of society.

In English, euphemisms are common in other taboo topics such as sex, physical and mental illness, and some bodily functions. Euphemisms are also common for certain jobs which are perceived as low status or unpleasant. For example, a *garbage man* may be called a *sanitation engineer* and a *rat catcher* may be called a *rodent operative*. The current word for the person who prepares a corpse for burial is itself a euphemism – *undertaker*. Although undertaker once meant 'someone who carries out any task', its meaning is now completely restricted to the tasks of burying the dead (although the verb *to undertake* has not been restricted in meaning in this way). Recently, some butchers in Great Britain have discussed adopting the euphemism *meat plant* for *slaughterhouse* and the Irish word *victualler* to replace *butcher*.[15] They are partly motivated by the desire to avoid the recent negative connotations of the word *butcher* when used to refer to particularly violent crimes of murder, e.g. the use of the phrase 'butcher of Lyon' to refer to Klaus Barbie, a Nazi held responsible for the torture and death of many Frenchmen during the Second World War. The source and motive for euphemism is the power of the connotations and associations that a word accumulates – the fact that words are affected by their context and collocations.

The effect on vocabulary is interesting. As one word acquires negative connotations, it is replaced by a new euphemism, which eventually acquires those same negative connotations itself. For example, the new phrase *funeral director* is preferred by some people (including those people who do this work) to *undertaker*, because the latter is acquiring negative connotations. In some cases the result has been a multiplication of words for the disagreeable. In English there are three words for 'bad smells' – *stink*, *stench* and *reek*. Each of these originally had a neutral meaning – the smell could be pleasant or unpleasant. Now they all mean exclusively bad smells. It is possible that the same change of meaning will happen to the word *smell*.

This process of *pejoration* – acquiring negative connotations and thus becoming degraded in meaning – is common in many areas of vocabulary. *Segregate* once meant 'keep separate', but because of the associations of racial and religious prejudice it now has negative connotations. *Exploit* once simply meant to 'use', without the idea of unfairness or selfish gain that it has now. A *pirate* was originally someone who 'tried' or took risks – an 'adventurer'. At one time, if you were *crafty* you were simply 'skilled'.

The opposite of pejoration is *elevation*. We have seen how the word *enthusiasm* became elevated. *Nice* is a particularly interesting example: it has changed from being a synonym for 'foolish', then 'particular', then 'affectionate' to its current meaning of 'pleasant'. In some cases terms for rank or position have changed meaning following a change in the nature of the office or position. A *minister* was once merely a servant of the king or queen; a *constable* was once a 'stable attendant'. Interestingly, elevation seems to be restricted to certain areas of vocabulary, notably religion and rank or position, whereas pejoration is common in a wide range of topic areas. The process of pejoration very often leads to the creation of euphemisms.

Slang

There are other terms in English for *to die* besides the ones listed above, but these are not euphemistic:

> to kick the bucket
> to turn up one's toes
> to hand in one's dinner pail

These expressions are *slang*, and unlike euphemisms they show a complete directness which seems to deliberately challenge the norms of society. The use of slang may show deliberate lack of dignity and rejection of the very existence of taboo topics. Whereas euphemism is formal, elevated language, slang is openly and sometimes aggressively informal and 'low status'. In other words, the use of slang says a great deal about the speaker's intentions. Language is being used to signal social attitudes.

Slang is also a group phenomenon – it can be used to signal group identity. Social groups are often very concerned with preserving their distinctness, and the special expressions of slang are a way of doing this. If someone does not know the slang of, say, rock music, this indicates to others that they are not a member of a particular group. Words such as *gig*, *hip-hop*, etc., are badges of group membership.

Another illuminating example is prison slang. Here are some examples of prison slang used in United States prisons: the slang expression *to dip* means to *eavesdrop*; a *castle* is the main prison in the capital city of the state; a *jeffer* is a new prisoner; a *solid dude* is a prisoner who has been in the prison for a long time and who has high status among fellow prisoners. Prison guards on the whole do not know slang (these examples were collected by a researcher at the University of Texas who had the trust of the inmates). If a guard tries to use slang in the presence of the prisoners, he will be laughed at and ridiculed. A study carried out in a US prison showed that the prisoners with the highest status among their fellow inmates were the most frequent users of slang expressions – for them it was a way of maintaining their status in the prison community.[16]

In certain areas of social life slang serves the function of a secret code. In the world of crime or illegal drugs it is important to have a secret language – such slang is usually very short-lived because it is a matter of survival to be able to tell the 'ins' from the 'outs'. Slang creates social distance as well as being a way of signalling group identity.

Jargon

Both euphemism and slang operate at the level of appropriateness in language. Whereas euphemism acknowledges the conventions of a society, slang can be used to reject them or to set up alternative conventions or ways of behaving. Euphemism and slang also contrast at the level of style – slang is informal, euphemism is formal. Jargon relates to these parameters in a different way. Jargon is used by high status groups and is often associated with professional terminology – computer jargon, medical jargon, etc. Like slang it is a *sociolect* – a variety of language used by a particular social group – and thus it identifies its members as a group. Unlike slang it does not convey rebellion or informality. An example from medicine illustrates these differences: a doctor may tell a nurse that a patient is in NAD, an abbreviation for the phrase *no acute distress*. This is professional jargon. But in hospital slang a patient who rings the bell for attention unnecessarily and constantly is a *bell-ringer*. Neither patients nor visitors would understand either of these expressions; both are part of the sociolect of doctors and nurses, but the former derives from medical terminology; the latter is unserious and informal in tone.

Scientific language is often the source of jargon, and in English this usually means the use of words with Latin and Greek roots. There can also be a strong element of euphemism in jargon. Two examples from the Vietnam War illustrate this point: *ambient noncombatant personnel* was a phrase used by the US military for *refugees*. Notice what aspects of being a refugee are being emphasised by this phrase: *ambient* – in the locality;

noncombatant – not involved in the fighting; and *personnel* – people with official or recognised status. These meaning elements do not accord very well with the homelessness of refugees and their need to escape from danger and destruction. The second example is also revealing. A US colonel once said to reporters at a news conference:

> You're always writing bombing, bombing, bombing – it's not bombing, it's air support.[17]

Clearly, in the mind of the colonel, dropping bombs from planes was a means of helping the military forces on the ground, and he was concerned that others should see it in that way as well. These phrases seem to make the act of bombing justifiable and the state of being a refugee less unpleasant. For this reason jargon is often criticised for attempting to hide the truth.

Each of these phenomena – euphemism, slang and jargon – shows that speakers can choose their words in order to show what social group they belong to, what attitudes they hold, how they view particular objects, people, actions, situations, etc. People make words work for them. In fact, they can even create new words to accomplish these same goals. We begin the next section by looking at how new words can be created in language.

Word formation processes

Let's begin this section by looking at a few examples of new words which have recently entered English:

fogeyish – the word *fogey* and in particular the expression 'an old fogey', meaning a person with old-fashioned ideas which he or she is unwilling to change, is itself not a new word. The etymology is unclear, but it may be that *fogey* is a form of the word *foggy*, which used to have as one of its meanings 'over-grown with moss'. Since moss only grows on stationary objects, such as stones (cf. the proverb 'A rolling stone gathers no moss'), *fogey* came to mean a person who 'doesn't move' (in ideas or attitudes). However, the form *fogeyish* is new – quite recently it was used in a newspaper article about advertising to describe ideas and attitudes about ethical issues in advertising which are beginning to be considered out-of-date.

harper – this word occurred recently in a newspaper article about musicians who play the Irish harp, which is a smaller instrument than the concert harp. English, of course, already has a word for a harp player – *harpist*. So why is a new word needed? According to the article the word *harpist* suggests the instrument used in a symphony orchestra and the playing of classical music. So, these musicians have wanted to create a

23

new word to refer to those who play folk music on these smaller types of harps. This is an interesting case of a new word being created because an existing word has certain connotations.

doorstep – the noun *doorstep*, meaning the area with steps leading to an outside door, is a well-established word, but recently it has begun to be used as a verb – *to doorstep*. It means to call at someone's house and talk to them standing on their doorstep in order to sell them something (a door-to-door salesman) or to get their opinion or support (as in political canvassing or market research).

In two of the three examples discussed above a new word has been created by changing the *form* of an existing word – by adding *-ish* or *-er*. In the third case, the 'sentence-building potential' of the word has been changed (without changing the form) so that it may be used in different types of grammatical structures. (After further discussion of sentence-building in Chapter Three, we will see that this involves a change of *class* – whether the word is a noun, verb, adjective, etc.)

Any native speaker of English is able to recognise by looking at the new form *fogeyish* that it is a descriptive word (an *adjective*), because of the final ending. Compare: *foolish, childish, squeamish*. Likewise, the ending *-er* in *harper* indicates that it is a noun which refers to a person or thing which does something. Compare: *play/player love/lover compute/computer*. Speakers of a language know how bits can be added to words to make other words – they know the rules of word formation in their language. The branch of linguistics which deals with the description of this knowledge – with the rules for word formation and the structure of words – is called *morphology*. Morphology means the 'study or science of form' and was first used in biology and botany. Here is a definition of its biological use from the *Oxford English Dictionary*:

> . . . that branch of biology which is concerned with the forms of animals and plants and the structures, homologies, and metamorphoses which govern or influence them.

Just as biologists study the various forms of, say, fruit-bearing trees, linguists study the forms of words. Let's look at English word formation processes in more detail.

Coinage

Interestingly, one of the most uncommon processes of word formation in English is the creation of totally new words which do not have any connection with pre-existing words in the language. The best examples are invented names for products, such as *nylon, aspirin* and *Persil* (the latter is a 'brand name' for a soap powder). The 1960s word *hippie* was

HERMAN   Jim Unger

formed from the word *hep* used in the 1940s but we don't know where *hep* came from – it could have been a totally new word.[18]

Borrowing

This process is one of the most common – words are borrowed from another language. We have already discussed the word *enthusiasm*, which was borrowed from Greek. It is possible to trace the borrowing of words through the centuries as English speakers came into contact with speakers of other languages, whether through invasion or conquest, or from incidental social contact. In the eighth century, waves of invaders came from Scandinavia to Britain. Words borrowed into English during this period include *skill*, *skin*, *sky* and many elements which have only survived in place names; for example, *-by* in Whitby and Derby comes from the Scandinavian word for *village*.

25

Although the Scandinavians did dominate Britain for a time, they eventually became absorbed into the native culture, and relatively few borrowings took place. However, the next major invasion was by the Norman French (1066), and they formed a socially and politically dominant class which ruled Britain for about three centuries. During this period many words were borrowed from French into English and this has had a lasting influence on the language.

Borrowing on a smaller scale can be traced from languages such as German (*rucksack, kindergarten*); Italian (*cantata, opera, concerto*); Indian languages (*shampoo, cot, juggernaut*). In this last case, it was the colonial domination of India by Britain which led to the borrowing.

Compounding

This process involves combining two or more existing words. Examples are *bookcase, textbook, doorknob, fingerprint, motorway*. Most compounds are nouns – they are formed because there is a need to name something which is newly invented or discovered or has not needed naming before, e.g. *motorway* or *desktop* publishing. A subtype of this process involves parts of words which are not in themselves independent words. An example is *graphy*, which has been combined with *photo-, calli-, biblio-*, etc. These forms come primarily from Latin and Greek, two languages which were viewed as superior to English in the fifteenth and sixteenth centuries. Although the idea that one language can be superior to another is fallacious, it did result in the use of many Latin and Greek combining forms as sources for word formation in English; *bio-, tele-, electro-* and *-scope* are just a few of the most common and productive forms.

Blending

Blending involves a type of combining, but in this process only parts of words are combined. For example, the *sm-* part of *smoke* has been combined with the *-og* part of *fog* to create a new word for a type of air pollution – *smog*. A recent example is the word *chunnel* to refer to the tunnel under the English Channel.

Clipping

Clipping, as the term suggests, involves removal – a word is made smaller. Either part of the end of a word is deleted, as in *exam, ad* and *fan* (*fanatic*), or a part of the 'front' of a word is removed, as in *bus* (from *omnibus*) or *plane*. *Influenza* and *refrigerator* have been clipped at both ends, producing *flu* and *fridge* (with a slight change of spelling in the latter example). These words are usually used in casual speech rather than formal speech or writing.

Acronyms

A new word can be formed by combining in sequence all the first letters of a phrase. In the case of proper nouns, the resulting word is usually written in capital letters (NATO, UNESCO). But in other cases we have what looks like a common noun, e.g. *laser* (light amplification by stimulated emission of radiation) and *scuba* (self-contained underwater breathing apparatus).

Conversion

This is the process which has been used to create *to doorstep*. Although no change in form takes place, a word which previously could only be used in certain ways to make sentences begins to be used in other ways, e.g. a word which was a noun becomes a verb also:

What a beautiful carpet!
We are going to have the hallway carpeted.

A very important category of word formation processes that does involve change in form is *derivation*.

Derivation

This process involves the addition of a small 'bit' to either the end or the beginning of a word: a prefix is a bit added to the beginning, and a suffix is a bit added to the end:

unhappy	kind**ness**
dislocate	fogey**ish**
misuse	harp**er**
resurface	ruth**less**
inhumane	child**hood**

Collectively, these are termed *affixes*. Some languages also use *infixes*, which are bits inserted inside a word. In Tagalog, a language of the Philippines, the infix /um/ meaning 'one who does' can be inserted into

the word form /pilit/ meaning 'effort' and this will produce the word *pumilit*, which means 'one who is compelled'.[19]

Derivational affixes can be described in terms of their function or meaning. For example, both *dis-* and *un-* have a negative meaning, and *-hood* has the property of making a word more abstract; for example, *child* is a common concrete noun, but *childhood* has the abstract meaning of 'condition or period of being a child'. If we examine some more forms of this word we can clearly see what elements of meaning are added by various affixes:

> childless – without children
> childlike – like a child
> childish – as above, but can have negative connotations

These derivational processes resemble conversion in that they may change the grammatical potential of a word, but unlike conversion, derivation involves a change of form. Here are a few more examples of the effect of derivational affixes:

> *-ation* this derives a noun from a verb
> to compute – computation
> *-ful* adds the meaning 'full of' and usually derives an adjective from a noun
> colour – colourful
> *-ment* usually derives a noun from a verb
> to place – placement
> *anti-* usually adds the meaning 'against'
> anti-terrorist
> *re-* adds the meaning 'again' or 'new'
> rethink

We can now introduce one more relatively minor word formation process – *back-formation*. This simply involves removing affixes, for example: *emote* (*emotion*), *enthuse* (*enthusiasm*), *televise* (*television*). In all these cases, one form of the word enters the language first, and another form is created afterwards.

Notice that although these affixes are meaningful elements just as the words they are attached to are meaningful, there is an important difference. Whereas *colour/think/place* can stand by themselves as single independent words, the affixes *ful/ment/re* cannot. In morphology a distinction is made between *free* elements (or independent elements) and *bound* elements. The term in linguistics for a minimal meaningful element is *morpheme* – so we have free morphemes (*colour/ think/ place*) and bound morphemes (*ful/ment/re*).

Free morphemes fall into two categories:

lexical morphemes – these are the words we think of as having meaning and therefore carrying the content of any message
functional morphemes – these consist largely of words which have a grammatical function, for example:
for but and when because on near above

(Although this is a useful distinction, it is obviously not a completely strict one – we can say that words like *because* and *near* carry meaning.)
Let's analyse a sentence using the categories introduced so far:

The doctor and his overweight patient talked about reducing his intake of sugar.
free lexical morphemes: doctor   sugar   overweight   intake
reducing   patient
free functional morphemes: the (twice) and   about   of   his
bound morphemes: -ed re- -ing

In the list of free lexical morphemes there are two words which are made up of other free lexical morphemes through compounding – *overweight* and *intake*. There is also an interesting complication in the word *reducing;* although *re-* and *-ing* are both bound morphemes, *-duc-* to which they are attached is *not* a free morpheme. In English it is usual that a bound morpheme is attached to a free morpheme (as *-ed* is attached to *talk*), so that every word is made up of at least one free morpheme. But here we have a word made up of three morphemes (*re/duc/ing*), none of which could stand on its own as a word – none is a *free morpheme*. In the case of *-duc-* we can find other morphemes with which it can combine to form lexical morphemes – *produce, induce, deduce* – but in some cases we cannot. For example, in the word *lukewarm* we clearly have two morphemes – *luke* and *warm*. The latter is a free morpheme; *luke* is bound – and it never occurs with any other morpheme to form an English word (we do not have *lukecool*).

Bound morphemes usually have a specific meaning, as was demonstrated by the list of derivational affixes given above. But in some cases it can be difficult to find a constant meaning for bound morphemes, and *-duc-* is a good example. It seems to have different meanings in words such as *induce, deduce* and *produce*. The information that it comes originally from the Latin word *ducere* meaning to 'lead', 'draw' or 'bring' is somewhat helpful – in *induce* something is 'brought in' or caused (e.g. What induced you to say that? His illness was induced by overwork). But this meaning doesn't seem to apply to the word *reduce*. Although this

29

word did once have a meaning 'to bring again' it has undergone a drastic change in meaning.

We have tried to use some basic categories to analyse a simple English sentence. But, as we have seen, there are many difficulties involved in describing the structure of words in English. The problems we have encountered are typical of those which linguists encounter when trying to describe the morphology of English or of any language: What categories need to be established? What are the rules in the language for forming words? What meanings do the morphemes in the language have?

We need to take our analysis of the word *talked* in our example sentence further. We have said that *-ed* is a bound morpheme, but it differs from the prefixes and suffixes we have discussed so far. This morpheme is not used in word formation in the same way as derivational affixes such as *-ful*, *-hood*, *re-*, etc. Instead, it is used to signal something about the grammatical meaning of the word *talked*. It tells us that this action took place in the *past*. This morpheme is an *inflectional* ending.

This brings us to the distinction in morphology between *derivational* morphology, which studies the ways a language has of constructing new words, and *inflectional* morphology, which studies the way words vary in order to express grammatical contrasts in sentences. The inflectional ending *-ed* on *talked* makes this verb into a past tense form. It is clearly a meaningful element – any verb with *-ed* has the meaning PAST TENSE added to it. We could show the process in a left to right diagram:

TALK	+	ED ⟶	*talked*
lexical morpheme		past morpheme	actual word form

Another inflectional morpheme in English is the plural morpheme. This adds the meaning 'more than one' to a noun:

BOOK	+	S ⟶	*books*
lexical morpheme		plural morpheme	actual word form

In these diagrams the capital letters have been used to show that we are dealing with abstract patterns in the language. Why we need to make this distinction becomes apparent when we examine such forms as *women*, *ran*, *gave* and *sheep*. The forms 'womans', 'runned', 'gived' and 'sheeps' do not exist in English, but we still want to say that, for example, the word *women* 'contains' the meaning PLURAL and *gave* the meaning PAST. We can represent the rules for their formation as follows:

WOMAN + PLURAL ⟶ *women*
GIVE + PAST ⟶ *gave*

These examples show clearly that English has more than one way to show plurality and past tense. To make a noun plural sometimes one needs to add the letter *s* to its written form, and another sound to its spoken form (e.g. *bag* has three sounds; *bags* has four). In some words different sounds are added, as in *ox/oxen*. But sometimes nothing is added – for example the plurals of *sheep* and *deer* are identical to the singular forms:

Look at that black sheep. There are ten sheep in the field.

To account for the complexity in English inflectional morphology, linguists must operate at an abstract level – their analysis of the structure of words needs to include abstract concepts such as *morpheme, past, plural,* etc. It is very useful to be able to say that there is an abstract plural morpheme in English which has a variety of *concrete* forms.

In this chapter we started by selecting words as units of the English language and looked at how linguists have attempted to account for the meaning of words. Then we examined how linguists have been able to discover patterns and thus describe the structure of words by analysing them into smaller abstract units – morphemes. We also saw how there are rules about combining morphemes. For example, certain derivational and inflectional affixes can be attached to forms to create different forms with different meanings. It is important to note that this cannot be done in a random way in English or any other language. For example, all English speakers know that *re-, big, -less* and *-ing* cannot be combined in that order to make a word. *Rebiglessing* is not English. It is the goal of the linguist to discover and make explicit the rules that all native speakers of a language know (albeit unconsciously) about the words of their language.

But as well as having knowledge about words, speakers of a language have knowledge about the sounds that make up those words. Consider 'pttska' – any English speaker would immediately react to this by saying 'That is not an English word, and could never be an English word – it just doesn't look or sound English'. In the next chapter we will examine the sounds of human languages and how linguists have described and analysed them.

References

[1] I am grateful to Verna Kilburn and her pupils for the use of their conversations

[2] F. de Saussure *A Course in Modern Linguistics* (Fontana 1974)

[3] D. Crystal *The Cambridge Encylopaedia of Language* (Cambridge University Press 1987)

[4] J. Swift *Gulliver's Travels* (Penguin) p.230

[5] Ogden and Richards quoted in Crystal (1987) p.101

6 J. Lyons *Language, Meaning and Context* (Fontana 1981) p.75
7 I. Leenhouts 'Towards a Taxonomy of Living Things in Teen' *Anthropological Linguistics* Vol. 29 No. 3 1977 p.313
8 The points in this section derive from S. Tucker's exhaustive study *Enthusiasm: a Study in Semantic Change* (Cambridge University Press 1972)
9 Tucker, p.30
10 Tucker, p.66
11 Bryom quoted in Tucker, p.70
12 Tucker, p.87
13 Tucker, p.85
14 Tucker, p.101
15 *The Guardian* 30 November 1984
16 These examples and analysis are from B. Little's study 'Prison Lingo: a Style of American Slang' *Anthropological Linguistics* Vol. 24 No. 2 1976
17 quoted in D. Bolinger *Language: The Loaded Weapon* (Harcourt Brace Jovanovich 1978)
18 H. Jackson *Words and Their Meaning* (Longman 1988) p.30
19 after Crystal (1987)

Chapter Two

Sounds

Phonetics

The branch of linguistics which has as its aim the description and classification of speech sounds is called *phonetics*. There are different branches of phonetics. Our main focus in this section will be on the way sounds are articulated – *articulatory* phonetics. Other areas within the study of phonetics are *acoustic* phonetics, which studies the physical properties of speech sounds as sound waves, and *auditory* phonetics, which approaches the study of sounds from the perspective of the hearer (also known as *perceptual* phonetics).

The first step in our study of articulatory phonetics is to identify what the organs of speech are – the *vocal* organs, and then to describe how these organs are used to articulate sounds. In order to do this, we will consider five sounds of English and examine which vocal organs are being used to produce the sound and what each *articulator* is doing in terms of position and movement. As each sound is analysed we will need to introduce the special phonetic symbol for it. It is vital for phoneticians to have a special set of symbols for sounds, because the letters used in writing systems often do not stand for one and only one sound. For example, in English the letter *c* in *cat* and *cease* stands for two different sounds. Other languages which also use the same alphabet as English does, use some of the same letter symbols for completely different sounds. If we compare the word for 'yes' in German and in English – *yes* and *ja*, we discover that both words begin with exactly the same sound, but German uses a letter *j* while English uses the letter *y*. The phonetic symbol is [j]. Phonetic symbols are always written with brackets surrounding them [ ]. Notice that the symbol [j] looks just like the letter *j* as in *ja*, so German speakers would probably find it quite easy to remember this particular phonetic symbol.

Sound One – *m*other (phonetic symbol: [m])
What happens when you make this sound? Probably the first thing

you notice is that the lips are pressed tightly together. So the upper and lower lips are vocal organs. Another point about the articulation of the sound [m] emerges if you try to extend this sound as long as possible. Soon you run out of breath, which simply means that sounds are produced using air from the lungs – an air stream is essential for producing sounds. Therefore, we can say that the lungs are also an organ of speech, although of course this is not their primary function. If an air stream is involved which begins in the lungs, then how does the air escape? It certainly cannot escape through the mouth when making [m], because the lips are tightly shut. Obviously it escapes through the nose. It travels from the lungs into the nasal cavity and out through the nostrils. This gives the sound a very special quality. Therefore, we have to consider the nose and nasal cavity to be another organ of speech.

Sound Two – *f*ather (phonetic symbol: [f])

The lips are also involved in the production of this sound but in a different way – the upper lip seems to be inactive as an articulator, but the lower lip is pulled back slightly and pressed very lightly against the upper front teeth, almost as if you were biting the lower lip. So the teeth are also vocal organs. (When young children loose their 'baby' teeth they often have trouble making certain sounds until their adult teeth grow in.) Now, how is the air from the lungs escaping? It is not escaping through the nose, because if you block the nose you can still make the [f] sound very easily. The air stream is escaping through the very small opening between the upper teeth and lower lip. This passage of the air stream gives the sound [f] a very different quality from the sound [m].

Sound Three – *s*un (phonetic symbol: [s])

The lips are not involved in the articulation of this sound (they are *passive articulators*), but the tongue is very important. The tip of the tongue is lightly touching the roof of the mouth just behind the upper front teeth. This area of the roof of the mouth is called the teeth ridge or the *alveolar ridge*. How is the air escaping? Not through the nose, but again through the very small space between the tip of the tongue and the alveolar ridge. Some air also manages to escape around the two sides of the tongue.

Sound Four – *z*oo (phonetic symbol: [z])

When you make this sound you notice that it is very similar to [s] in articulation – the tongue is in exactly the same position. Try saying the word *zoo* and then the word *Sue* immediately afterwards. You use the same tongue position at the beginning of both words. So what makes these two sounds so different? Notice that the [z] sound has a vibrating or buzzing quality that [s] does not have – [z] even sounds just a little bit louder than [s]. The source of this buzzing noise is in the throat. It is the larynx. The larynx is perhaps the most important organ of speech. Inside the larynx are the vocal cords. These can be brought close together so that when air from the lungs passes through them they vibrate in much the same way that the mouthpieces of musical instruments such as clarinets and oboes do. This vibration produces the buzzing sound known as *voice*. If you rest your hand on the front of your throat you may even be able to feel the vibration of the vocal cords as you produce the sound [z]. The sound [s] does not have this quality – it is therefore known as a *voiceless* sound whereas [z] is a *voiced* sound.

If we go back to Sound Two [f], notice that it does not have this vibration quality, but the sound [v] as in *vote* does. The sounds [f] and [v] are made with the articulators in exactly the same position – the only difference between them is that [f] is voiceless and [v] is voiced. What about Sound One [m]? It also has this buzzing quality – it is voiced.

Sound Five – *y*ellow (phonetic symbol: [j])

The tongue is the most active articulator in the production of this sound. In producing [j] the middle area of the tongue (not the tip) is pressed lightly against the middle of the roof of the mouth. This area of the roof of the mouth is quite hard because there is bone underneath (there is also bone underneath the alveolar ridge). The phonetic term for the roof of the mouth is the *palate*. Towards the back of the mouth the palate becomes much softer (there is no bone underneath) – this area is known as the soft palate or *velum*. It is the velum that is responsible for directing the flow of air either through the nasal cavity or through the mouth (the oral cavity). The velum is actually a muscle which can be flexed or relaxed. When it is relaxed the air from the lungs can pass over it into the nasal cavity and out of the nostrils, as happens when you are breathing normally or making a sound such as [m]. When it is flexed it blocks the passage of air into the nasal cavity and the air is forced to flow out through the mouth, as it is for [f], [s] and [z]. In the case of the sound [j] the air is also stopped from flowing into the nasal cavity and flows out through the mouth. You may be able to notice that the middle of the tongue is not pressed very tightly against the hard palate when you make [j]; in fact, there is a small empty space at the very centre point of the hard palate and the sides of the tongue are pressed tightly against the inside surface of the back teeth. This means that the air can easily glide over the centre of the tongue and out through the mouth. This gives the

[j] sound a very distinctive quality – quite different from [f] or [s]. We can now review all of the vocal organs in Figure 2.1:

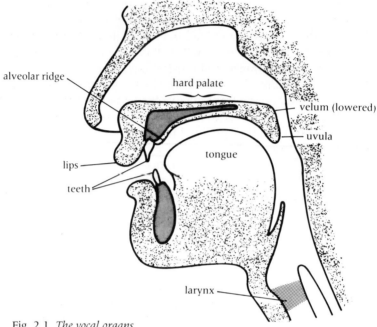

Fig. 2.1 *The vocal organs*

The description of sounds

In the description of the above five sounds of English we saw that the air stream is directed or affected in many different ways by the articulators – the lips can block air flow through the mouth, the teeth and tongue can form a small space through which the air has to squeeze out, etc. So, one important aspect of the description of sounds is *where* they are made – in phonetics this is termed their *place of articulation*, that is, the location where the air stream is being most modified and the precise articulators involved in that modification. The following is a list of the possible places of articulation:

Bilabial sounds

These are sounds made with both lips. The initial sounds of the words *pig* and *big* are both bilabial sounds. Our Sound One [m] is a bilabial sound.

Labiodentals

These are sounds formed with the upper teeth and the lower lip. Our Sound Two [f] is a labiodental sound, as is [v].

Dentals

As the choice of label would suggest, these are sounds made using the teeth, specifically the front teeth. What happens with this type of sound is that the tip of the tongue is placed against the front teeth and the air is squeezed through the space that remains. In English there are two dental sounds – the sound at the beginning of the word *that* [ð] and the sound at the beginning of the word *thick* [θ]. (Notice that the only difference between these two sounds is that the first one is voiced and the second [θ] is voiceless.)

Alveolars

Sound Three [s] is an alveolar in place of articulation because the tip of the tongue is placed against the alveolar ridge. In English there are several alveolar sounds: the initial sounds in *tip*, *dig*, *not*, *lot* and *rot* are all alveolar sounds, so with [s] and [z] English has seven alveolar sounds.

Palatal

These are sounds which are located at the hard palate, and it is the tongue which is principally involved in their articulation. Sound Five [j] is a palatal sound in English. Italian has a slightly different palatal sound in the word for 'son' – *figlio*. In Italian this sound is usually spelt with the letters –*gli*–; the phonetic symbol for this sound is [ʎ].

Alveolar–palatal

Although English has only one palatal sound, it has four sounds which must be described as alveolar–palatal. This is necessary in order to give a precise definition of their place of articulation. The sounds are: 1) the sound at the beginning and end of the word *church* [tʃ]; 2) the sound at the beginning and end of the word *judge* [dʒ] (notice that there are two different spellings in English for this sound – the letter *j* and the letters *dg*); 3) the initial sound in *shape* [ʃ], which is usually spelled with the letters *sh*; 4) the sound in the middle of the words *treasure* and *vision* [ʒ], which is spelled with the letter *s*.

Velars

These are sounds produced quite far back in the mouth at the velum. The sounds at the beginning of the words *good* and *cook* are velar in place of articulation. They are produced by lifting the back part of the tongue so that it briefly touches the velum. The other velar sound in English is the sound at the end of the words *ring* and *bang* (as these two examples show it is usually spelled with the sequence of letters *-ng*). The phonetic symbol is [ŋ], which almost looks like a combination of the letters *n* and *g*.

Uvular

The *uvula* is the term for the very tip of the velum, and sounds can be made with the back of the tongue touching it. English has no sounds which are uvular in place of articulation, but many other languages do, for example there is a uvular sound in Arabic, and both French and German have sounds which have this place of articulation.

Glottal

All the places of articulation we have discussed so far involve the action of the tongue and other parts of the mouth. But it is possible to produce sounds at other locations. The space between the vocal cords in the larynx is called the glottis. During normal breathing, the air can flow freely through the glottis. This simple sound of breathing can also be used in languages. In English the initial sound [h] as in *house, heat* and *who* is produced in this way; however, there is usually a narrowing or constriction at other points in the mouth for each [h], so there actually are glottal sounds in English which differ slightly. For example, in the word *heat* notice that you make the [h] sound as you are getting ready to make the next sound; in the word *house* you make the [h] sound while you are getting ready to make the sound spelled *–ou–*, so these two [h] sounds are slightly different.

There is another way to make a sound at the larynx – you can shut the vocal cords very tightly and then open them again very quickly. The sound produced is very sharp and quick, almost like a soft cough. The phonetic symbol for this sound is [?]. It occurs in many languages, but in English it is only used in certain accents.

These phonetic labels allow linguists to describe sounds in terms of where they are made. But as we have seen from the examples above, it is possible for different sounds to be made at the same place of articulation, so obviously place of articulation does not provide us with a full and complete description of the sounds of speech. We must also give information about *how* sounds are made. One aspect of sound production that has already been mentioned is the voiced–voiceless distinction. All speech sounds are either voiced or voiceless. As we have seen above, in English and in many other languages there are pairs of sounds which are alike except for the fact that one sound is voiced and the other voiceless, for example, [s] and [z], [f] and [v], etc.

Sounds also differ in their *manner* of articulation, that is, in the action and coordinated movements of the articulators and how this affects the flow of air from the lungs.

Manner of articulation

Stops

It is possible for the articulators to interrupt the flow of air from the lungs. For example, to make the sound [d] as in *dog*, you press the tip of the tongue tightly against the alveolar ridge, making sure that the sides of the tongue are also pressed tightly against the back teeth. You hold this position and the air from the lungs builds up slightly to create pressure in the oral cavity. Then you quickly release this pressure and the air explodes sharply through the mouth. (Another term for this type of sound is *plosive*.) This manner of articulation produces very quick, abrupt sounds. In English, there are six stops or plosives: [b] as in *buy*, [d] as in *dig*, [g] as in *go* (all voiced), [p] as in *pet*, [t] as in *two* and [k] as in *keep* (all voiceless).

Fricatives

Sounds Two, Three and Four ([f], [s], and [z]) are all fricative sounds. This manner of articulation involves a partial blocking of the air stream so that the air must squeeze through a small opening between the articulators. For example, in the sound [s] the air must squeeze between the tip of the tongue and the alveolar ridge. As the air is pushed past the articulators by the force of the lungs, a sound of friction or 'hissing' is produced, hence the term fricative.

Affricates

If you combine an interruption of the air stream with a release which causes a friction sound, the result is an affricate sound. When you make the sound at the beginning of the word *chew* you assume the position for the stop [t] and then release the air using the friction-producing position for the fricative sound [ʃ] (the sound in *shoe*).

Nasals

Our Sound One was a nasal. The velum is lowered so that air flows through into the nasal cavity and out through the nostrils. Some air may try to flow into the mouth but there is a total obstruction there so that it cannot escape and must be 're-routed'. In the case of the sound [m] it is the lips that form the obstruction in the oral cavity; in the case of the sound [n] it is the tongue tip and sides which form the obstruction; for [ŋ] it is the back of the tongue. English has three different nasal sounds (labial [m], alveolar [n] and velar [ŋ]). There are many other nasal sounds in other languages. All have air flow through the nose, but each has a different point of total obstruction in the mouth (its place of articulation) – this determines the quality of the nasal sounds. For example, Spanish has a palatal nasal, which sounds quite different from the labial, alveolar and velar nasals of English.

Liquids

The initial sounds of *lot* and *rot* are commonly described as liquids. The term itself suggests the smooth quality of the sounds. This quality is due to the fact that the articulators involved are quite loosely held together. Unlike fricatives, no friction is produced – instead the air escapes fairly freely.

Glides

This category of sounds is very similar to liquids in that the air flow does not become violent because of total or partial obstruction. They are thus very similar in quality to vowels, where, as we shall shortly see, the air flow is hardly restricted at all.

To sum up, we have seen that in order to give a thorough description of the physical aspects of speech sound production, the science of articulatory phonetics must use various descriptive labels. For each sound we want to describe we need to say:

1) whether the sound is voiced or voiceless
2) what the place of articulation is
3) how the sound is being produced – the manner of articulation.

By referring to air flow, action of the larynx, and the position and movements of the vocal organs, phoneticians can describe any speech sound used in any language in the world. The categories listed above are essential for the description of the consonant sounds of speech because these always involve some sort of constriction or obstruction (all the example sounds given so far have been consonant sounds). Below is a list of the consonant sounds in English. Afterwards, we will look at the way that vowel sounds can be described.

/p/	top	bilabial stop voiceless
/b/	bee	bilabial stop voiced
/t/	two	alveolar stop voiceless
/d/	do	alveolar stop voiced

/k/	car	velar stop voiceless
/g/	go	velar stop voiced
/tʃ/	watch	alveolar-palatal affricate voiceless
/dʒ/	joy	alveolar palatal affricate voiced
/f/	fun	labiodental fricative voiceless
/v/	vote	labiodental fricative voiced
/θ/	thick	dental fricative voiceless
/ð/	the	dental fricative voiced
/s/	so	alveolar fricative voiceless
/z/	zoo	alveolar fricative voiced
/ʃ/	shoe	alveolar-palatal fricative voiceless
/ʒ/	vision	alveolar-palatal fricative voiced
/h/	have	glottal voiceless
/l/	lot	alveolar liquid voiced (air passes over the sides of the tongue)
/r/	rot	alveolar liquid voiced (air passes over the centre of the tongue)
/m/	me	bilabial nasal voiced
/n/	no	alveolar nasal voiced
/ŋ/	ring	velar nasal voiced
/j/	yes	palatal glide voiced
/w/	won	labio-velar glide voiced

The description of vowels

Unlike consonant sounds, vowel sounds are not produced by creating barriers to air flow with the tongue, teeth or lips, or by bringing the vocal organs very close together so that a friction sound is produced as the air flows through. Instead, a space of a particular shape is produced in the oral cavity, and it is this characteristic shape of what is actually a resonating chamber that gives each individual vowel its particular quality. For example, for the vowel in *beat* a space shaped like a curved narrow tube is made in the mouth. But for the first vowel in *father* the tongue is lowered and pulled back and the mouth opened fairly wide to give the large space needed for this vowel's quality. Even a very small change in the configuration of the lips and tongue produces a different shape and therefore a vowel sound of different quality. Try making the vowel sounds in *heat* and *bit* and notice how little the tongue moves from making one to making the other.

It is quite difficult to be consciously aware of the different shapes used to make vowel sounds, but one feature of vowel production which is fairly easy to notice is lip position. In Figure 2.2 there are four drawings of the lip positions for four of the vowels which are used in English, the vowels in:

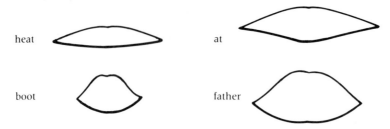

heat

at

boot

father

Fig. 2.2 *Lip positions in the production of vowel sounds*

For the vowel in *heat* the lips are spread apart, very like a smile; for *boot* the lips are pursed and rounded, as in whistling; for *father*, the lips are quite far apart; and for *at* they are slightly spread, the corners of the mouth being pulled back. These are the four extreme lip positions for the production of vowels – in making any other vowel, the lips will assume a position somewhere within these four extremes.

Manner of articulation for vowels is very easy to describe. All vowels are made with unimpeded flow of air; all vowels are voiced in all languages in the world (with some exceptions). What about place of articulation? Instead of using the places we identified for consonants, we are able to describe all vowel sounds by using classifications based on how close the tongue is to the roof of the mouth, and whether the tongue is pulled back or pushed forward. As we have seen, position of the tongue and the lips determines the size and shape of the space created inside the mouth and this gives each vowel its special sound quality.

Say the word *father* and concentrate on how you make the first vowel. Notice that for the first vowel in *father* the tongue is flattened, quite far from the roof of the mouth, and pulled towards the back of the mouth. The first two classifications are BACK and LOW. For the vowel in *beat* the tongue is positioned towards the front of the mouth, very near the front teeth, in fact, and quite close to the roof of the mouth, so we have FRONT and HIGH (sometimes the term CLOSE is used instead of HIGH). In making the vowel sound in *get* the tongue is mid-way between a HIGH and LOW position (MID) and the tongue is towards the front of the mouth, so *get* has a MID FRONT vowel. The vowel in *saw* is MID also, but the tongue is further back, so this vowel is MID and BACK.

We also have a middle point between FRONT and BACK which is CENTRAL. In English the second vowel in the word *father* is a CENTRAL vowel. These labels can be used to describe the vowels of any language. The dimension of lip position is usually described by saying that a vowel is ROUNDED or

UNROUNDED. For example, the vowel [i] as in *beat* is UNROUNDED but the vowel [u] as in *two* is ROUNDED. In Figure 2.3 there is a list of some of the vowels in English and their positions on a grid marked with the labels FRONT, BACK, etc.

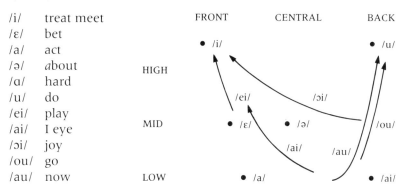

/i/	treat meet
/ɛ/	bet
/a/	act
/ə/	*a*bout
/ɑ/	hard
/u/	do
/ei/	play
/ai/	I eye
/ɔi/	joy
/ou/	go
/au/	now

Fig. 2.3 *A grid showing place of vowel articulation*

In the list in Figure 2.3 the symbols have been written between slanted lines / /, instead of brackets [ ]. (This notation was also used in the list of consonants.) This indicates that the vowels and consonants are being treated not as physical sounds but as units in a language, in this case, English. There are twenty-four consonant sounds in English and sixteen members in the vowel system. (There are of course different accents of English, and one of the ways these accents are distinctive is that some use a slightly different set of vowel sounds. We will be examining these differences at the end of the chapter; for now we will consider sixteen as a kind of 'basic' vowel inventory for English.)

Notice that the last five vowels in the list contain two symbols within the lines and have been located on the grid with directional arrows. These symbols represent the start and finish points for these vowels; these five vowels are made by changing the position of the articulators during the production of the vowel instead of holding a particular steady position. They are called *diphthongs*; the other vowels are called *monophthongs*.

Phonology

In the previous section we have seen how sounds can be described using various categories: voiced, high, fricative, etc. These categories can be used with reference to any language, although we have been using examples taken from English. If we narrow the scope of description to particular languages, then the first thing we notice is that each language makes a selection from the full range of possible sounds which can be produced by the vocal organs. No language uses anywhere near all of the possible sounds that human beings can produce.

Secondly, sounds are combined in language to form meaningful words but this combining is done according to strict rules. Not all combinations are allowed in a particular language. For example, the following is not a permissible combination for English: [tpon], but it might easily be permitted in another language. These two aspects of sound selection and combination are central to the study of sound patterns in a language. Phonology is the branch of linguistics which is concerned with the description of the patterns of sounds in a language and the way the set of sounds in a particular language works as a *system.*

Units of phonological analysis

In order to describe the organisation of sounds in a language, we must have some basic units. One of the important units in phonology is the syllable. Most people seem to be able to say, without much difficulty, how many syllables a given word has and (perhaps with more difficulty) where one syllable ends and the next begins. Some writing systems devised for languages are actually based on the syllable – they make use of a syllabic script.[1] This in itself is evidence that the syllable is an important unit.

If we take the syllable as a unit, we can analyse its structure in order to see if there are patterns of formation and organisation. All syllables seem to have a core or a *nucleus* and marginal elements which follow and precede the nucleus. The nucleus position is usually taken by a vowel sound, and some syllables contain only a nucleus. For example, the English word *a*, and the Russian word for *and* [i], and the first syllable of the English word *even* (*e–ven*) have only a nucleus.

There can be an articulatory element following the nucleus, which cuts down or stops the flow of air and brings the syllable to an end. The following English words have just one syllable with a vowel nucleus and a consonant sound which follows the vowel:

> ate   eat   oat   an   on   of   it   up

Preceding the syllable core or nucleus there can be another marginal element. These English words of one syllable have a nucleus and a preceding element:

> to   low   lie   ray   me   sigh   tea   no

(It is vital not to confuse number of sounds with number of letter symbols – all of the above examples have two sounds only, even though some of the words have more than two letters, e.g. *tea* has three letters in its spelling but two sounds: /t/ and /i/.)

The following words have *both* marginal elements – one before the core and one after it:

> coat   Kate   beat   ban   run   bed   lip   pet   nut

We see from these examples that there are three positions or 'slots' in a syllable. Only one of these is obligatory (the core or nucleus), the others are optional. It is also clear from the examples that the nucleus position is occupied by a vowel and the marginal elements are occupied by consonants. So a syllable is made up of sounds that can stand on their own or are at the centre of a sequence of sounds; and sounds that cannot occur on their own, or are at the edges of a sequence of sounds. The 'independent' slot – or the core – can be given the label 'v' (it is usually vowels which occupy this position), and the marginal slots can be given the label 'c' (it is usually consonants that occupy this position). Using these labels we can describe the structure of syllables in the following way:

(a symbol 'o' is used when a particular slot is not occupied)

of	ovc	at	ovc	go	cvo	bit	cvc	a	ovo
she	cvo	put	cvc	me	cvo	top	cvc	oh	ovo

Using this notation to represent the types of syllable structures, it is possible to compare different languages. From the examples above we see that English has all four types cvo, cvc, ovo and ovc. Other languages do not: for example, Hawaiian has only two types, ovo and cvo.

How would we analyse the structure of the English word *plum*? This is a monosyllabic word, just like the other examples above, but its initial slot is filled by two consonants, not one. It has the following syllable structure:

> letter symbols: p   l   u   m

sounds:	/p	l	ʌ	m/
structure:	c	c	v	c

If we examine more monosyllabic words in English we find that there are quite a few possibilities for the marginal positions:

streets	cccvcc	blast	ccvcc	free	ccv	found	cvcc
split	cccvc	its	ovcc	smooth	cccc		

However, the possibilities are limited. The largest number of consonant sounds at the beginning of an English syllable is three and the largest number allowed at the end is four (although there are only a few words that have that many – one of them is *twelfths*). We can write a formula which reflects these restrictions:

$$c_{0-3} \quad V \quad c_{0-4}$$

This simply says: 'English can have one, two, or three consonants in the syllable initial position and one, two, three, or four in syllable final position'. Again we can compare different languages. Chinese, for example, can only have four types of syllables: ovo, cvo, ovc, cvc. This means that its formula is:

$$c_{0-1} \quad V \quad c_{0-1}$$

Arabic can have two consonants together, but only in final syllable position:

$$c_{0-1} \quad V \quad c_{0-2}$$

This aspect of sound patterns explains why some sequences of sounds are 'impossible' as English words. All English speakers would react immediately to the sequence 'pttska' by saying 'That doesn't look or sound English'. The reason is simple – it does not conform to the rules for syllable structure in English because it has too many consonant sounds in the initial position.

We have discussed one aspect of syllable structure in languages, the size of the consonant groups that are permitted in syllable initial and syllable final position. There are also restrictions on which consonants can occur together in these groups. Look at the following list of monosyllabic words:

play	bleed	close	glow	pray	breed	tray	drive	crow
grow	twin	dwell	pure	cute				

Each of these words has two consonants in initial position. Of these two consonants, the first is a stop, either /p/, /b/, /t/, /d/, /k/, or /g/. Now notice that the second consonant is one of four, either /l/, /r/, /w/, or /j/

(the first three are represented by the letters *l*, *r* and *w*; notice that in *pure* and *cute* there is a /j/ sound after the first consonant although this sound is not represented in the spelling of these words). This is a strict rule in the syllable structure of English; we can express it as follows:

> When a syllable has two consonants in initial position, and the first consonant has the manner of articulation *stop*, then the second consonant must be either /l/, /r/, /w/, or /j/.

This rule means that there are no words in English that have either two stop consonants in initial position, e.g. /tpon/, or two fricatives, e.g. /sfot/ or two liquids, e.g. /rlip/. These are impermissible sequences in English.

But there is a further restriction: according to the rule above, we should have words such as /pwik/ or /bwed/ or /tlip/ or /dlet/ in English, but we do not. What is happening? If we refer to the chart of consonants showing place of articulation, we see that both /p/ and /b/ are bilabial and that /w/ is also bilabial. It seems that English does not use consonant initial groups beginning with a stop which has the same place of articulation as the next consonant. The rule is very consistent: /t/ and /d/ are both alveolar and they cannot be followed by an /l/ which is also alveolar. This pattern is specific to English; there are other languages which do not have these restrictions. An example is Tlingit, which is spoken in Alaska. The name of this language shows that it does not have a restriction against the sequence /tl/!

Comparative phonology

Equipped with an understanding of the ways in which languages use sounds, linguists can compare the characteristics of different sound systems. The University of California at Los Angeles is the home of a survey of the sound systems of 317 languages (UPSID – University of California Phonological Segment Inventory Database). Not all the languages of the world were included, but a representative selection was made with members of each of the different language families (e.g. West Germanic, Indo-Pacific, Polynesian, etc.).

Several interesting tendencies and patterns emerge. For example, 70 per cent of the languages surveyed had between 20 and 37 sounds in their inventory; the largest inventory discovered was 141 and the smallest only 11. When the inventories were analysed into types, it was found that consonants were far more common than vowels: the average number of consonants was 22.8 and the average number of vowels was 8.7. However, there are some languages that have more vowels than consonants – one of the Indo-Pacific languages has 12 vowels and 10

47

consonants. One of the American Indian languages has 46 consonants and only 3 vowels.[2]

All languages in the UPSID survey have stop consonants and of these, voiceless ones occur more frequently than voiced. Most languages have stops at three or four places of articulation. Bilabial stops, dental or alveolar stops, and velar stops are by far the most 'preferred' – over 99 per cent of the languages in the survey had stops at these places of articulation.[3]

The majority of the languages surveyed have up to four fricatives, but some have as many as twelve. The most frequent fricative is alveolar /s/ – 83 per cent of languages have this sound. Next comes /ʃ/ and /f/, then /z/. By far the most frequent nasal sound is /n/. Some languages only have one nasal, but if there is a second nasal it is /m/. Only four languages in the whole sample had no nasal at all.

There seem to be no cases of languages with only one vowel, but we have seen that one language in the sample had just three. Most languages seem to have between five and seven vowels.

Another abstract unit

In comparing languages we have studied the sound inventories. What we have not included in these inventories are the variations in the set of sounds that occur when people speak. For example, when English speakers say the words *keep* and *caught* /kip/ and /kɔt/, they actually make two different kinds of /k/. In the word *caught* the sound at the beginning of the word is voiceless, stop and velar. But there is a slightly different sound in the word *keep*. Instead of being velar, as it usually is, this /k/ is actually palatal in its place of articulation – the tongue is further forward in the mouth. The phonetic symbol for the palatal voiceless stop is [c].

But we do not want to say that the sound [c] is part of the basic inventory of English – it is simply a variant of the sound /k/ which occurs in certain circumstances. In fact it is possible to describe very exactly what those circumstances are. The variant of /k/ is used whenever there is a following vowel which is produced in the front of the mouth – a FRONT vowel. Remember that the back of the tongue is used in producing velar sounds, so it is almost as if the speaker knows that a sound produced in the front of the mouth is coming next and he or she gets ready for it, 'anticipates it', so the tongue is pulled slightly forward in the mouth and a palatal consonant is produced instead of the more usual velar sound. This behaviour is very consistent among speakers of English, and because this variant of /k/ can be predicted we do not want to say that it is a member of the inventory of English. Instead we say that the basic members of the inventory are phonemes, and that sometimes there are variants – called *allophones* – of these phonemes.

Phonemes and allophones

Let's look at a few more examples of phonemes in English and their allophones.

The phoneme /t/. When English speakers pronounce /t/ at the beginning of a word, they release the closure between the tip of the tongue and the alveolar ridge in such a way that a puff of air accompanies the sound. This puff of air is known as aspiration. But in words in which the /t/ phoneme is preceded by an /s/ as in the word *stop*, English speakers make the sound in a different way: they do not add the aspiration. English speakers don't notice that they are doing this; it is part of their unconscious control of the pronunciation of their language. In fact, if someone, let's say a foreigner learning English, pronounced the word *stop* and used an aspirated version of /t/ the English listener would probably not notice the difference, but would still recognise the word as *stop*. This pronunciation might sound slightly strange to an English ear, but it would not make any significant difference.

There is another variety of /t/ that some English speakers use. Instead of producing a sound which is voiceless, alveolar and a stop, they produce a glottal stop (see list of places of articulation). This happens in words where the /t/ phoneme is surrounded by vowels, as in the word *butter*. So the variant is completely predictable. When an English listener hears this pronunciation it does not cause any problems. The use of the variant does not make any difference to the identity of the word. We can say that the unaspirated /t/ and the glottal stop are allophones of the phoneme /t/.

The theory of phonemes and allophones can be used to explain some of the difficulties people encounter when they learn a new language as adults. When people learn their native language, they soon learn which sounds are phonemes and which are simply variants, and in what circumstances the variants are used. When they try to learn another language, it may happen that a sound which is just a variant (an allophone) in their language is not simply a variant in the second language. It actually makes a difference to the identity of the word. For example, in English the sound /ʃ/ is pronounced slightly differently in the word *shoe* than it is in the word *she*. English speakers will round the lips while making the sound /ʃ/ in *shoe*; in pronouncing *she* the lips will not be rounded. If an English speaker were trying to learn Lak, spoken in the Caucasian Mountains in the Soviet Union, he or she would have to learn that /ʃ/ with lip-rounding and /ʃ/ without lip-rounding are two different phonemes. This might be a very difficult distinction to control because in English these sounds are simply interchangeable.

Distinctive feature analysis

In examining the sound inventories of languages and the phoneme/ allophone distinction we have been treating sounds as units. But the science of phonetics clearly demonstrates that sounds are not indivisible – we can think of the sound /s/ as having the features voiceless, fricative and alveolar. In other words, we can talk in terms of bundles of features. When we do this it is easy to show that some sounds resemble each other very closely and other sounds do not share any features at all. If we take the two sounds /s/ and /z/, we can present them as collections of features. The sound /s/ is voiceless, alveolar and fricative, or:

$$
/s/ \\
\begin{bmatrix} -\text{voice} \\ +\text{alveolar} \\ +\text{fricative} \end{bmatrix}
$$

(The plus and minus symbols work as a shorthand to say that the sound either has the feature (+) or does not (−).) If we do the same analysis for /z/:

$$
/z/ \\
\begin{bmatrix} +\text{voice} \\ +\text{alveolar} \\ +\text{fricative} \end{bmatrix}
$$

we see that these two sounds differ in only one feature, voicing. But the two sounds /z/ and /p/ differ in all features:

$$
/p/ \\
\begin{bmatrix} -\text{voice} \\ +\text{bilabial} \\ +\text{stop} \end{bmatrix}
$$

The analysis of sounds into features is very similar to componential analysis – the analysis of words into meaning components (see Chapter One). If we use this way of analysing sounds it is possible to see some patterns in the sound system of a language. Let's look again at the two pronunciations of /ʃ/ in English as in *shoe* and *she*. What reason might there be for the pronunciation difference in the consonant – is it simply an accident or a whim? If we examine the features of each of the sounds a possible explanation emerges. Let us look at the features of the vowels (the vowel in *shoe* is /u/ and the vowel in *she* is /i/:

$$
\begin{array}{c}
/u/ \\
\begin{bmatrix}
+\text{voice} \\
+\text{high} \\
+\text{back} \\
+\text{round}
\end{bmatrix}
\end{array}
\qquad
\begin{array}{c}
/i/ \\
\begin{bmatrix}
+\text{voice} \\
+\text{high} \\
+\text{front} \\
-\text{round}
\end{bmatrix}
\end{array}
$$

How is /ʃ/ pronounced when /u/ is the next sound? We saw that the variant involved rounding of the lips. If we check the feature analysis for /u/ we see that it is also +round – the two sounds share this feature. So we have a possible explanation: /ʃ/ is pronounced with rounding of the lips when it immediately precedes a vowel sound which also has lip rounding; if the next sound does not have lip rounding (as /i/ does not) then there is no 'matching up' of features. We say that one sound *assimilates* – becomes more similar to – another. It seems that the neighbouring sounds in a word influence each other. In phonology we can write rules to show what is going on. The rule that describes the above pattern would be written as follows:

This rule can be read as: 'The consonant /ʃ/ becomes rounded before a rounded vowel'. The arrow symbol has the meaning 'becomes' and the line __ indicates the relative position of the two sounds – in this case the __ is in front of the vowel sound and this shows that this change comes about when the consonant is in front of the vowel. Notice that this rule makes explicit exactly what is happening – a feature is being added to a sound which is the same as a feature of the following sound. Rules of this form, although they look complicated, are able to describe exactly what is happening to sounds in a language – phonological processes.

Phonological processes

Here is another example of assimilation and how rules that represent sounds as bundles of features can reveal general patterns. The example comes from Portuguese. In Portuguese words, when a vowel sound is followed by a nasal consonant, the manner of articulation of the vowel changes. The vowel becomes nasalised, that is, as well as air flowing out through the mouth, air also flows out through the nose, so the vowel becomes more similar to the nasal consonant. Since this happens to any vowel which precedes any nasal consonant we can write a rule using a small set of distinctive features:

$$\left[+\text{vowel}\right] \longrightarrow \begin{bmatrix} +\text{vowel} \\ +\text{nasal} \end{bmatrix} \bigg/ \underline{\hspace{1cm}} \begin{bmatrix} +\text{consonant} \\ +\text{nasal} \end{bmatrix}$$

So far we have given examples of assimilation of place of articulation and manner. Let's look at one more example – of voicing assimilation.

Imagine a language in which the vowel sound /u/ was added to a word to show that it was plural. So if the word 'tup' meant one book, then 'tupu' meant two or more books. Here are two more imaginary words:

'mut' mirror   'mutu' three mirrors
'fot'   box   'fotu'   many boxes

Now we give some information about pronunciation: 'tup' is pronounced [tup] but 'tupu' is pronounced [tubu]; 'mut' is pronounced [mut] but 'mutu' is pronounced [mudu]; and 'fot' is pronounced [fot] but 'fotu' is pronounced [fodu]. Notice what happens to the consonant at the end of the word when the vowel [u] is added – it changes from voiceless to voiced. Now we know that vowels are usually voiced, so the process seems to be one of assimilation of voicing – when a voiceless consonant is between two voiced sounds it becomes voiced. Using distinctive feature analysis we can explicitly describe this process:

$$\begin{bmatrix} +\text{cons} \\ -\text{voice} \end{bmatrix} \longrightarrow \begin{bmatrix} +\text{cons} \\ +\text{voice} \end{bmatrix} \bigg/ \begin{bmatrix} +\text{vowel} \\ +\text{voice} \end{bmatrix} \underline{\hspace{1cm}} \begin{bmatrix} +\text{vowel} \\ +\text{voice} \end{bmatrix}$$

Now that we have explored the way that the sounds of languages are produced and organised, we can return to some observations about the structure of words in Chapter One. Remember we saw that there are various ways of making nouns in English plural. Sometimes there is a *zero* ending (as in *sheep*); sometimes there is a change in the vowel sound (*man/men, foot/feet*); but the most common pattern is *hat/hats, dog/dogs*, etc. In writing, the change is a very simple one – the letter *s* is added to the end of the word. But what sound is added in speech? If you pronounce the two plurals above and listen carefully to the last sound, you will observe that in *hats* it is /s/ (a voiceless alveolar fricative) and in *dogs* it is /z/ (a voiced alveolar fricative). This is confirmed if other plurals are examined:

maps   buns
bits   seeds
books   sounds
puffs   leaves

Why do some nouns add /s/ and some /z/? And how do English speakers know which to choose? The answer is simple – all we need to do to find out is to look at the last sound in the singular form of the noun. If it is voiced then the voiced /z/ is added; if it is voiceless then the voiceless /s/ is added. The rule works for words ending in vowels as well – all vowels in English are voiced, so /z/ is added to make the plural of nouns which end in a vowel: toe/toes sea/seas way/ways eye/eyes.

But we don't yet have the complete picture – what about words where *es* is added in the spelling? These are pronounced with an 'extra' syllable: bushes churches cruises branches   masses. All the words that add a syllable in their plurals have either /s/, /z/, a fricative, or an affricate sound at the end of the singular form. It seems that a rule of sound sequences is operating here – English does not permit a sequence of two fricatives or a fricative and an affricate in its syllable structure, so a vowel sound is added to break up this impermissible sequence whenever it occurs (as happens when forming the plurals of words like the above.)

Summary of points

In this chapter we have examined some of the basics of sound production and how the study of phonology focuses on how sounds operate as a system. The phonology of a language includes restrictions on the sequences of sounds in a language. Each language has an inventory of sounds, its phonemes, and there are variants of those sounds which are predictable, the allophones. Distinctive feature analysis allows us to explain some of the patterns in pronunciation in terms of processes, such as *assimilation*. In the next section we will look at some of the ways that sounds and pronunciation are used by speakers in talking – 'in action'.

Sounds in action

We have discussed variation in sound production and variation in sound systems; in this section we will explore the role of these in accent variation. There are many accents in English – the definition of an *accent* is 'features of pronunciation that identify regional or social groups'; in other words, accent is related to a person's identity. English accents differ in several ways. We have already mentioned the use by some speakers of the glottal stop – this sound is used both by certain speakers from Scotland, e.g. Glasgow, and by some speakers in London (in particular speakers of Cockney English). As an example of accent variation and its significance to English speakers, we will investigate the /r/ sound and the 'meaning' it has for speakers of English.

In Scotland, many speakers pronounce an /r/ sound that is made by striking the tip of the tongue very quickly several times against the alveolar ridge – this type of sound is commonly known as a 'trill'. In some parts of the north of England, an /r/ sound is produced at the back of the mouth – to be precise, it is a uvular trill. The /r/ sound used at the beginning of words by many speakers in the United States is slightly different from that used by speakers in the south of England – the American version has a slightly different tongue position. Speakers of English in India, i.e. speakers of Indian English, may use an /r/ sound which is like a short tap – instead of the tip of the tongue striking the alveolar ridge several times, as in the Scottish trill, there is one quick tap. These are some of the regional differences that exist, and English speakers are very sensitive to them. In fact, if an English speaker notices that the person they are speaking to pronounces their /r/ in a different way, this helps them to tell where that person might come from.

But another aspect of the /r/ sound is whether it is pronounced at all after vowel sounds. No speakers delete an /r/ sound at the beginning of a word, such as *run* or *rich*, but after a vowel sound many speakers do delete the /r/, for example, in the words *matter* and *more*. In fact, one can set up a basic distinction between those speakers who pronounce *postvocalic* /r/ and those who do not. It is often said that speakers of English from England 'drop their /r/' and that American speakers 'pronounce the /r/'. In the United States, it is said that /r/-pronouncing accents are the norm, and people associate r-less pronunciation with the Southern States and parts of New England. But as we shall see, the situation is much more subtle and complex than these generalisations would seem to suggest.

One important factor in the r-less or r-full pronunciations in Britain is that there is an accent which is considered to be the national prestige norm in England and Wales. This accent is known as Received Pronunciation or RP for short. RP is not a regional or local accent. It is distributed throughout these two countries through the highest social classes. RP has been described in the following way:

> RP has . . . remained the accent of those in the upper reaches of the social scale, as measured by education, income and profession or title. It is essentially the accent of those educated at public schools (which are, of course, private, and beyond the means of most parents). It is largely through these schools that the accent is perpetuated.[4]

It is also the accent associated with broadcasting and with the centres of education (Americans have a tendency to call it 'Oxford English').

RP is an r-less accent, and this has implications for the way English listeners react when they hear a pronunciation which deletes the postvocalic /r/. This feature of pronunciation is considered to carry *prestige*.

In the Eastern States in the US, the situation is quite different. For example, in New York City the pronunciation of /r/ after a vowel is considered to be a prestigious type of pronunciation, and r-lessness is non-prestigious. This pattern was clearly shown by studies carried out in New York City by the sociolinguist William Labov in the 1960s.[5] He was convinced that the way New Yorkers pronounced words with /r/ 'in the spelling' clearly revealed the attitudes people held about differing forms of speech and different groups of people – their *stereotypes*.

Previous studies of New York speech had claimed that sometimes New Yorkers pronounced the /r/ sound and sometimes they didn't – their behaviour was random and insignificant. Labov set out to show that this was an oversimplification and that the meaning of r-less pronunciation was being obscured. After collecting a large number of tape recordings of New Yorkers, his research seemed to show that there was a pattern in the pronunciation of /r/. Labov concluded that New Yorkers considered it to be a sign of social prestige to pronounce the /r/ sound after vowels, so that when they were being careful about their speech they pronounced more /r/s. There was thus a stylistic pattern. There were also differences in social class. In general, people from a lower class background used fewer /r/sounds in their accent.

Let us look at another example of how features of pronunciation are seen to have high or very low prestige by speakers of a language. A feature of the Cockney accent of London (which originated in the East End of the city) is that words beginning with an *h* are pronounced without this /h/ sound. So a Cockney would say 'I've lost my 'at, can you 'elp me find it', omitting the initial sounds at the beginning of the words *hat* and *help*. Many people in Britain react quite violently to this feature of pronunciation – they condemn it as slovenly and careless and very low prestige. Cockneys are condemned for 'dropping their h's'. When people react this way they are actually using this feature of the Cockney accent as a symbol for the negative image that many people have of people from the East End of London. One stereotype of Cockneys is that they are cunning, somewhat dishonest and uneducated. At the same time there are very positive features of the Cockney stereotype – they are seen to be friendly, quick-witted and warm-hearted. Many Cockney speakers take great pride in their distinctive accent and would never think of trying to change it; others share part of the negative stereotype and may actually try to lose this highly stigmatised feature of their speech. But when people condemn speakers for not pronouncing the *h* sound at the beginning of words, they are more often than not using pronunciation and accent as a means of expressing social attitudes towards certain groups of people.

CULTURE FOR THE MILLION; OR, SOCIETY AS IT MAY BE.

REPRESSION OF HABITUAL CRIME.—B. A. 1 (*to Benevolent Old Gent.*). "WHAT'S HE 'BEEN AND DONE?' WHY, HE'S BEEN AND DROPPED AN H! THAT'S WHAT HE'S 'BEEN AND DONE!' ISN'T THAT ENOUGH?"

This has been a very brief survey of some of the findings of recent research which show that accents have a social meaning for people. The way a person speaks is a part of their identity. This is demonstrated by the way some people react when they move from one part of the English-speaking world to another. Even after living in their new home for many years, some speakers will still keep their accent. It is almost as if accent is used as a badge of identity, a signal of social group membership.

References
1. Some examples of languages that use syllabic scripts are Japanese (kana), Amharic, and Cherokee.
2. reported in D. Crystal *The Cambridge Encyclopaedia of Language* (Cambridge University Press 1987) p.165
3. D. Crystal (1987) p.166
4. A. Hughes and P. Trudgill *English Accents and Dialects* (Edward Arnold 1979) p.2
5. see for example W. Labov *The Social Stratification of English in New York City* (Center for Applied Linguistics 1966)

Chapter Three

Sentences

In the first chapter we saw how linguists study the formal variation of words – morphology. Another main focus in grammatical analysis is the *behaviour* of words. We can compare what a linguist does when studying language with what a chemist or zoologist or botanist does when studying natural or synthetic substances, animal life, or plant life. A chemist designs and carries out experiments in order to find out how particular substances behave: At what temperature does gold melt? Will sulphur combine with water? Biologists study animal behaviour: Why do cranes leap in the air? Why are coelacanths only found at the bottom of the Indian Ocean? How do birds know when to migrate? Linguists are interested in syntactic behaviour – in the distribution of words, in their combinatory properties, in the order of words in a sentence, and, of course, in their differences in form, as we have already seen. Their data are the sentences of a language, the sentences that people have actually spoken or written or that they judge to be possible sentences in English. Also, an important part of their data are the sentences that do not belong to English (or whatever language is being studied). What doesn't happen is just as important as what does happen – both are part of the linguist's data.

The behaviour of words in sentences

If we examine the following phrases we see that the words *nice* and *happy* behave in the same way:

he's nice   she's happy   the nice boy   the happy girl

If we look at the distribution of the two words we find that both can occur in two positions: 1) after the word *is* and 2) between the word *the* and a word such as *boy* or *girl*. We have identified two contexts or 'environments' for *nice* and *happy* – they fit into specific slots or frames.

is _____   the _____ boy/girl

We can now use our 'frames' to test more data:

the happy child	*the already boy
the nice man	*the some man
the sad mother	*the through mother
*he is were	*she is greedily

(the symbol * before a sentence or phrase indicates that it is not well-formed)

Our test frames show that *happy, nice* and *sad* behave in the same way; and that *already, some, through* and *greedily* do not share this aspect of behaviour. Based on our analysis we can set up a class of words in English and give this class a label – the class of *adjectives* or *modifiers. Happy, nice* and *sad* are members of this class; all of the other words we have tested are not.

The establishment of classes has always been central to grammatical study. Dionysius Thrax was a Greek grammarian who lived in the first century B.C. In the history of the Western tradition of linguistics he is often given the status of 'founding father'.[1] He established classes of words for Greek which he termed 'parts of speech'. Two of the classes he established were *nouns* and *prepositions*, and he devised the following definitions for them:

> The noun is a part of speech inflected for case, signifying a person or a thing.
> The preposition is a part of speech placed before other words in composition and in syntax.

Notice that the definition Thrax gave for prepositions is based on position. This definition of the class *preposition* would appeal to modern linguists because it refers to the behaviour of prepositions. Thrax's definition of a noun includes a reference to the morphology of nouns in Greek – they were *inflected* for case. However, modern linguists would argue with the remainder of the definition of noun because it includes semantic meanings – '. . . signifying a person or a thing . . .'. In English, it is easy to think of words which clearly belong to the class of nouns because of their syntactic behaviour, but do not signify a person or a thing. *Sleep* and *help* are examples, as in the sentences 'Sleep is essential for good health', 'I need more sleep', 'I need some help'. These nouns clearly do not signify a person or a thing but an activity. There are of course many nouns in English and other languages which do signify persons and things, and this is one reason why the class label *noun* is still used in modern linguistics. But syntactic behaviour is the primary criterion used by modern linguists in establishing classes. In some cases formal criteria – the inflectional endings a word may have, such as *-ed*,

-*ing*, -*s*, can be used, but in English not all word classes show differences in form, so ultimately linguists must rely on syntactic behaviour. Modern linguistics does not find descriptions of language which rely on loose explanations based on meaning satisfying, just as modern biology does not find explanations of animal behaviour like 'Cranes dance because it is their nature' satisfying.

Some word classes in English

In this section we will examine three word classes in English. Our focus will be on the structural features which 'signal' or give information about the way these groups of words behave. The linguist's goal is to set up classes that are 'coherent'. If we discover that we have included in a particular class a word or group of words which behave somewhat differently in certain respects from the others, this means we must rethink our classes.

The word class 'personal pronoun'

Let's start with the class of personal pronouns. The members of the class of personal pronouns in English are as follows:

I   me   we   us   you   he   him   she   her   it   they   them

It is interesting to note that the pronouns of English haven't changed for three centuries.[2] This is very different from the class of nouns, for example. We have seen in Chapter One that this noun class is con-tinuously acquiring new members – 'newly coined words' – and grad-ually losing other members, as words become 'obsolete'. So the first observation we can make about the class of pronouns is that it is a 'closed' class, in contrast to other classes which are 'open' classes.

The following sentence has eight personal pronouns:

I know that you agree with me but he doesn't, nor does she, and so we must try to persuade them to support us or they will be a threat.

Imagine you overheard this utterance, as you walked past a room or picked up the telephone. Even though you had no idea what the conversation was about – except that it involved an issue on which people disagreed – the pronouns used by the speaker provide a lot of information about the people involved. Firstly, they provide information about the participants in the conversation. The pronouns *I* and *me* refer to the speaker, whereas *you* refers to the hearer or *addressee*. In contrast to the pronouns which refer to participants, *he* and *she* refer to people who are not participants in the conversation. The speaker's use of pronouns serves to identify persons in terms of their relation to the speaker – are they being addressed by the speaker or not? The people referred to by the words *he* and *she* may be present in the room (although most people who overheard this would probably assume that they were not) but the speaker does not identify either of them as being *hearers*. In a conversation, when one person finishes speaking and another person begins, the 'new' speaker will use *I*, *you*, *he*, etc., to identify participants and non-participants – speaker, addressee(s), and 'other parties'. The exact reference of the two *participant* roles – *I* and *you* – changes with each new speaker.

Secondly, the choice of *he* and *she* conveys certain information about the non-participants. We know immediately that the person referred to as *he* is male and the *she* is female. Notice that if someone overhears this utterance, there is no information available about the sex of *you*. Nor is the sex of the speaker shown by the word *I* in English (the only clue might be whether the voice of the speaker sounded like a male voice or a female voice).

How many people are being spoken to? Obviously *I* is one person – there is one speaker, and a listener would know that there are two individuals who disagree with the speaker (the *he* and the *she*). But what about *you* – how many addressees are there? This is problematic. Unless the participants are seen, it is impossible to tell how many people are being addressed – there could be just one or more than one. The pronoun *you* in English can be 'singular' or 'plural'. In other languages there are separate pronouns for one hearer or more than one. In Annatom, a language of Melanesia, there are separate personal pronouns for you–singular (*aiek*); you–two (*aijaurau*); you–three (*aijautaij*); and *aijana* for addressing more than three people.[3] Older forms of English had special dual pronouns: *wit* meant 'we–two' as in 'hwaet wit gespraecon' (what we–two said) and *git* meant 'you–two'.[4] Some modern varieties of English have a separate you–plural form: in the southern part of the United States 'you all' is used when addressing more than one person. If, however, the speaker continued talking and said the following sentence, the listener *would* know whether there was just one addressee or more than one:

> I'd like you to ask yourself whether you think this is important enough for you to help me.

Anyone who overheard this utterance would know that the word *you* referred to one person because of the following word *yourself* – this is a singular form. The plural form is *yourselves* (I'd like you to ask yourselves whether . . .).

The pronouns *we*, *us*, *them* and *they* also have reference to more than one. They are all plural. But there is an ambiguity in the use of *we*. It is possible that when the speaker says *we*, the word *we* means the addressee and the speaker together. But it is also possible that *we* means the speaker and one or more non-participants and excludes the addressee. For example, *we* could mean the speaker and the members of a certain group to which the *you* does not belong. *We* always refers to the speaker, but it may *include* or *exclude* the addressee(s). The same is true of the pronoun *us*. This distinction is sometimes called *inclusive* or *exclusive* reference. For example, in 'Shall we dance?', *we* obviously includes the addressee, who would be astonished if the speaker suddenly began to dance alone. But in 'We enjoyed your lecture' the addressee (the lecturer) is excluded – *we* refers to the speaker, plus another person or persons who heard the lecture. So, a simple statement that *I* means a single speaker and *we* means more than one speaker is inaccurate. *We* is occasionally used when people speak in unison, for example, at a football match where spectators shout 'We want a goal' or after a popular performance, when the audience may shout together 'We want more'.

This examination of the sentence shows that, in English, pronouns operate according to *number* (reference to one, or more than one), *person* (reference to speaker/hearer(s), i.e. the participants, and the non-participants), and *gender* (the sex of the people referred to). By 'operate' we mean that there are formal variations that signal these distinctions, e.g. the different forms *he*, *she*, etc., and that other parts of sentences in which pronouns occur behave in response to the number, person and gender of the pronoun. For example, if the speaker had said 'She agrees with me, and he agrees with me, too' the verb in the sentence would have an -*s* ending to match with these non-participant pronouns. All other pronouns would not require an -*s* ending (I agree, we agree, they agree, etc.).

In working on the grammar of a language, linguists establish analytic categories such as number, person and gender. These are three examples of what are usually called *grammatical categories*. Of the three we have looked at, person is termed a *deictic* category (deixis means 'pointing') because it is used to identify or indicate objects, people, etc. in relation to the speaker in place and time. Part of the linguist's task is to discover how each word class behaves with respect to the set of grammatical categories.

The word class 'noun'

The next example of a word class is the class of nouns. One simple observation is that nouns, like pronouns, operate according to number. Nouns can be plural or singular. In Chapter One we have seen how the morphophonemic rules for number operate in nouns in English. To begin our analysis of the word class *noun*, let us look at some of the differences in the ways nouns and pronouns behave:

Pronouns do not occur with *the, a, this* (determiners)[5]
　　　　　　　*the you　　*this me
Nouns do occur with determiners – the boy　this child

Pronouns have an objective case i.e. in 'He asked her and then she asked him' the forms her and him are used for the receiver of the action of asking
Nouns show no differences in form for case – 'The boy asked the *girl* and then the *girl* asked the man.'

Pronouns have a distinction for person (*I* versus *you, you* vs. *they*, etc.)
Nouns show no distinction in person

Pronouns show a contrast in gender – *he–him* vs. *she–her*
Some *nouns* show gender differences through morphological endings – *waiter/waitress　host/hostess　hero/heroine* but others do not – *brother/sister　king/queen*

Pronouns have singular and plural forms which are not morphologically related e.g. *I* and *we* are completely different forms
In *nouns*, the singular and plural forms are morphologically related – *boy/boys　girl/girls　house/houses*[6]

Noun sub-classes

We have compared and contrasted the syntactic behaviour and form of two word classes in English – nouns and pronouns. But within the word class of nouns, there are groups of words which behave differently, in other words, there are noun sub-classes in English.

Here is a selection of some English nouns:

word　finger　grass　progress　sunshine　bottle　cup　harm
book　letter　symbol　wood　butter　water　weather　furniture
leather

This group contains two different types or sub-classes of nouns, but we can't tell which word belongs to which by looking at the words. In English, we cannot identify sub-classes of nouns on the basis of *form*, but syntactic behaviour does lead us to establish sub-classes. Let us look at the differences in syntactic behaviour of nouns in English, using the words in our list as examples.

First of all, some of these nouns can occur with numerals in English sentences:

    one word   one cup   one bottle
    two words   two fingers   three cups

If the numeral is 'two' or higher then the noun gains an inflectional ending to show plurality (see Chapter One).

However, in the case of other nouns, we cannot use them with a numeral or attach the plural morpheme:

    *one furniture   *one weather
    *two harms   *three weathers

Secondly, the group that can occur with numerals or have the plural form can also occur with the determiner *a(n)*:

    a word   a finger   a cup   a bottle

but the other group cannot:

    *a grass   *a furniture   *a weather   *a sunshine

If we check the co-occurrence of nouns with the determiner *some*, we find that we can have:

    some grass   some sunshine   some harm   some progress

but we cannot have:

    *some word   *some cup   *some bottle   *some finger

We can only use *some* with members of this group if we make them plural:

    some words   some cups   some bottles etc.

Based on this evidence, there are two sub-classes of nouns – the first group contains:

    word   finger   cup   bottle   book   letter   symbol

They can be made plural and can occur with *a* but not with *some* in the singular. They are usually called *count* nouns or *countable* nouns. They refer to discrete objects which can be counted. The other group are usually called *mass* nouns:

    grass   furniture   weather   sunshine   harm   leather   progress
    wood   water   butter

They refer to an indivisible substance e.g. sugar, grass, sand, which is somehow thought of as a collection. If we want to refer to a discrete part of these collective mass nouns, we need to use another noun to make a phrase, for example:

grain of sugar   blade of grass   grain of sand   piece of furniture
ray of sunshine

Notice that if we do this, we can then 'count' these items e.g. 'There are several expensive pieces of furniture in the room' or use them with numerals – 'The small insect weighed as much as three grains of sand' or use the phrase with the word *a* – 'The feather was as thin as a blade of grass'. However, by themselves, this group of nouns behave in a very distinctive way. The important point to remember is that there is nothing about the form of English nouns that shows whether they are members of the *countable* sub-class or of the *mass* sub-class. A particular noun can only be identified as mass or count by examining the syntactic behaviour of the word. For these reasons, many traditional grammars of English ignored the count/mass distinction in nouns. But this exclusion was a serious flaw because native speakers have, as part of their internal knowledge about English, knowledge about mass and count nouns. The knowledge they have is unconscious – they do not have to consciously think about whether it is permissible to add *-s*, use the noun with *some* in the singular, etc. It is one part of their knowledge of the system of English.

Although the count/mass distinction is not signalled by variation in form, modern linguists still want to say that count/mass is a grammatical category (just like *person* and *number*) in English, because it is a useful distinction in describing the grammatical system of English and because their goal is to represent everything the native speaker knows (consciously and unconsciously) about the English grammatical system. The following rule can be used to represent the distinction between the sub-class *count noun* and the sub-class *mass noun*:

$$\text{N} \longrightarrow \begin{Bmatrix} \text{N (count)} \\ \text{N (mass)} \end{Bmatrix}$$

This rule simply says 'Any noun in English belongs to the class mass or the class count'.

Before we can build sentences in English which have plural nouns, or which have the determiner *a* or the word *some* we need to 'select' the nouns we want to use and check which class each noun belongs to – count or mass. For example, if we want to build a sentence with the word *coffee* we must first identify this as a mass noun. This will then 'prevent' us from using the word *a* before *coffee* in the sentence. Native speakers will do this unconsciously, but the set of grammar rules linguists construct for English must reflect these unconscious decisions explicitly.

Some puzzles and some explanations
But some strange things can happen with mass and count nouns in

English. One of these is that some mass nouns can sometimes behave exactly like count nouns. Here are a few examples of sentences which seem to ignore the mass/count difference, and yet are perfectly grammatical sentences in English:

> We have a selection of coffees and teas for you to choose from.
> I'll have a coffee.
> I'd like a juice.

Also, some nouns seem to belong to both sub-classes:

> We need some light in here. (light – mass noun)
> We need some lights in here. (light – count noun)
> The talks on arms control begin tomorrow. (talk – count noun)
> I dislike silly talk. (talk – mass noun)

There are various ways to explain these sentences. We could say that in English there are two separate nouns, say, *talk* (mass) and *talk* (count). With many of the nouns that seem to be both mass and count, the mass noun has a more abstract meaning, and the count noun has a more concrete (and thus countable) meaning. Consider the sentence: 'Light travels faster than sound' where *light* is viewed as an abstraction. But in the sentence, 'We need some more lights in here', *lights* are viewed as physical objects – we could replace the word *light* with *light fittings* or *lamps*. In sentences in which a mass noun is behaving like a count noun, as in 'I'd like a coffee', we could say that the phrase 'a cup of' has simply been omitted from the sentence. Everyone who has studied the French Revolution knows of Queen Marie Antoinette's reply when she was told that the poor people of France were rioting because they did not have enough bread to eat. In English translation, her reply is 'Let them eat cake'. In English, *cake* can be used as a mass noun – referring to a type of food, or it can be used as a count noun – referring to individual items of that type of food, e.g. 'We need to buy three cakes for the party'. There is a semantic difference, just as there is between *coffee* as a type of beverage made from beans grown in tropical countries and a particular amount of the liquid brewed and served in a cup. The following sentence combines both meanings:

> Coffee is a stimulant, so it is unwise to drink more than three coffees a day.

Many food nouns in English behave as count nouns when they refer to a particular item and behave as mass nouns when they refer to the article of food as a type of food. The following sentence shows the same kind of difference:

Talk between colleagues should always be constructive, but all the talks I have had with him have made the situations worse.

The level of meaning cannot be ignored and, in the case of nouns, this involves the way items are perceived by people. We think of certain substances – water, butter, sunshine, etc. as indivisible. In English, these perceptions have become part of the grammatical system, so linguists need to establish mass/count as a grammatical category. In analysing any language, linguists must recognise three inter-related levels[7]:

the level of form
the level of grammar
the level of meaning

The next word class we will examine is the class *verb*. In this analysis we will examine, in turn, the different forms of the verb in English (the level of form). As we look at form we will relate it to the grammatical category of *tense* (the level of grammar). And we will look at the meanings of each form as they relate to the concept of time (the level of meaning).

The word class 'verb'

First we examine verb forms with the *-ed* ending:

Verb + -ed

The co-occurrence of *-ed* verb forms and phrases or words which refer to past time (e.g. *yesterday, last year*, etc.) demonstrates clearly that there is a correspondence between events in the real world that are past at the time of speaking and the use of a verb form with *-ed*. Corroborating evidence comes from the fact that the following are ungrammatical sentences:

*I called him tomorrow.
*Next week I saved a lot of time.

These observations show that the grammatical category of *tense* is relevant to English, and furthermore that one of its members is *past*. To be complete, our description of past verb forms must also include the fact that forms such as **goed *buyed *gived *thinked* do not occur in English, but that the forms *sent bought gave thought* are used. We have seen in Chapter One that we need rules such as the following to convey this information:

GO + PAST ⟶ went
CALL + PAST ⟶ called

and a more general rule to tell us that past is part of the category of tense in English:

Tense ⟶ {Past}

67

Complications

But things aren't quite so simple and straightforward. There are some cases where a past tense verb form is used but there is no implication of past time. Reported speech is a good example: Imagine my sister, Jan, says to me one morning: 'I plan to be back home late this evening. Please tell Mother.' When I report this fact as requested, I would say 'Jan said she planned to be back home late this evening' – 'planned' certainly doesn't refer to a past event. Past tense forms are also used when describing unreal situations – 'I wish I knew what to do' or 'If only I understood the problem, then maybe I could help'. The word *could* is an example of the most extreme case of non-correspondence between past tense forms and past time. The group of six verbs in English known as the modal auxiliary verbs have two forms:

can	could
will	would
shall	should
may	might
etc.	

The forms in the second column are usually referred to as the past tense form in traditional grammars, and in some cases they are used to refer to past events. For example, 'When I was young, I could speak Spanish, but I can't any more – I have forgotten everything'. However, the forms *could, would, might*, etc. are more often used in other ways. The statistical analysis of the occurrences of *would* in a recently collected computer data base for English show this very clearly.[8] Out of 14,687 occurrences of the word *would* 48 per cent were uses of the word 'to talk of events which are of a hypothetical nature at the time of speaking' as in 'What would you do in my place?'. Eight per cent of the cases were used for the conditional: 'If you would help, I'd appreciate it'. Twenty-one per cent of the occurrences were used to refer to past time, but note that there is a restriction here – *would* is used to refer to past habits only. It is an alternative to using the phrase 'used to' ('Every morning he would go for a run'). Six per cent of the cases were in reported speech, and, as we have said above, this use cannot really be considered to be a reference to past time. So only about one-fifth of all occurrences of *would* have anything to do with past time. This is true of the other forms as well; for example, *should* is often used for giving advice.

So there are complications – not all past tense forms correspond to past time, but it is clear that past tense verb forms very frequently correspond to past time although the correspondence is not exclusive. However, we still need to establish a category of *tense* for English and to identify one of its terms as *past*. It is important to remember that *tense* is a grammatical category – a level of description – an abstract notion that linguists set up to explain how English verbs work.

Now we turn to the verb forms with the auxiliary *have*. This verb form is complex – not only is there the word *have* (or *has* when the subject is a single 'non-participant' – *he, she,* or *it, the President, Mary, my friend,* etc.) but the verb must be in a particular form. For most verbs this is an *-ed* ending (*painted, walked, reported*) and for some it is an *-en* ending (*broken, eaten,* etc.) Some of the *-en* group also have a different vowel (*fallen,* etc.).

$$\left\{ \begin{array}{l} \text{ha ve} \\ \text{has} \end{array} \right\} \quad \text{Verb} \quad \left\{ \begin{array}{l} \text{ed} \\ \text{en} \end{array} \right\}$$

The following sentences show that this form cannot occur with words or phrases which indicate past time:

*George has broken his arm $\left\{ \begin{array}{l} \text{last week} \\ \text{two days ago} \\ \text{last month} \\ \text{in 1976} \\ \text{long ago} \end{array} \right.$

It does co-occur with expressions such as:

$\left. \begin{array}{l} \text{At present} \\ \text{Now} \\ \text{So far} \\ \text{Up till now} \end{array} \right\}$ I have eaten three biscuits.

But past tense verb forms cannot occur with the above expressions:

*So far I ate three biscuits.   *Now I broke my arm.

Clearly, the two verb forms have different uses. But there are some expressions that can occur with both forms:

Jim has fallen off his horse
    fell off $\left\{ \begin{array}{l} \text{today} \\ \text{this week} \\ \text{recently} \\ \text{this afternoon} \\ \text{before (now)} \end{array} \right.$

So the past tense *fell* and the *have -en* form obviously share something at the level of meaning. Both forms are used to talk about events that are past in time, but the *have* form (usually called the *perfect*) looks at these past events from the perspective of the present. If we look at the phrases which can be used with the *have -ed/en* form we see that they all refer to an interval of time which includes both the time of the past event, and the present – the time of speaking. 'Today' is an interval of twenty-four hours. If Jim fell off his horse at 10.30 am and I report this to someone at 3.00 pm the word 'today' includes both times. The same is true of 'this century': 'There have been many developments in medicine this century'. The developments are past events, but they are viewed from the perspective of the present moment – both points in time are included in the phrase 'this century'. The use of *have -ed/en* forms includes a present-time perspective; in some explanations of the English verb system the term 'current relevance' is used.

Next we examine the *-ing* forms of verbs. Like the forms of the verb with *have* we have just discussed, the *-ing* forms are also complex:

> The baby is crying.
> John is sleeping.
> I am reading *War and Peace*.
> We are eating dinner.
> I am watching my favourite television programme.

$$\left\{ \begin{array}{l} \text{is} \\ \text{are} \end{array} \right\} \quad \text{Verb} \quad \left\{ \text{-ing} \right\}$$

We see from these examples that a form of the verb *to be* occurs (in the above examples it is *is* or *are*) plus a verb with an *-ing* ending. What time reference do we have in these sentences? Clearly there is a starting point for each action sometime in the past. But the actions have not finished – they continue into the present. We might ask 'When did the baby start crying?' or 'When did John fall asleep?' and the answers would be a point of time in the past. But the questions, 'When did the baby stop crying?', 'When did you finish *War and Peace*?' are unanswerable. It is clear that *-ing* forms of the verb can be used to talk of continuing actions that extend over a period of time, and in these examples the activities are still progressing at the present moment.

Of course, if the action or activity was continued over a period of time in the past and has finished, we can communicate this by combining past tense and *-ing* forms:

> I remember exactly what happened last night. John was sleeping and I was watching my favourite television programme. Then the phone rang.

Notice that it is only the *to be* part of the verb that changes into past tense. There is no form of the verb 'was slepting' or 'was watcheding'.

But again, as with the past tense verb forms, there are cases where the

-ing form is not used to refer to actions in progress. It is often used to talk about future time:

> I am leaving for Spain tomorrow.
> I am going to give up smoking.

To complete our examination of verb forms in English we must look at forms of the verb such as:

a) I like whisky.
b) He leaves for work at 7.30.
c) I don't care.
d) My coffee is cold.
e) Water freezes at 0 degrees C.
f) Plants need light.
g) We aren't ready.
h) He needs help.
i) A watched pot never boils.
j) He has a new car.

There is an *-s* ending on the verb when the singular non-participant pronouns or a noun occur (*he, she, it, pot,* etc.) and there are two forms for BE (*is* and *are*) and two forms for HAVE (*have* and *has*). In sentences like j) the verb HAVE is not an auxiliary but a full verb with the meaning close to 'possess'. Otherwise, the basic form of the verb is used. In traditional grammar this simple form of the verb is usually called the *present tense*. But the correspondences with present time are not at all straightforward or clear. We could certainly add the words *now, at the present time* or *at this moment* to c), d), g), h) and j) to demonstrate that these sentences are really referring to present time, but in cases like b) this description is inaccurate. These are more accurately described as habitual actions. To show this we can add phrases like *all the time, everyday, regularly*. In the case of e) and f) the statements clearly do not refer to any particular time, but are simple statements of truth. This is shown by the fact that if we try to make these sentences refer to past time ('Plants needed light and water') some crucial element of meaning is lost.

So-called *present* tense forms are also used to refer to 'states' or 'conditions'. For example: 'He is kind and gentle/ I love you/ I am happy /I know'. We can also make a distinction between inherent states, such as 'He is kind' and resultant states, such as 'My coffee is cold' (the temperature of the coffee is a result of some action, e.g. it has been left in a cold place).

All of this evidence seems to indicate that whereas we can clearly establish the term *past* in the grammatical category of tense for English,

71

there is not such strong evidence for the term *present*, because this would not reflect the facts about how these forms are used. While there is a frequent and direct correspondence between past tense forms and past time, there is not the same kind of correspondence between 'so-called' present tense forms and present time. Instead we will use 'past' and 'non-past' for the category of tense in English. The following rule represents this:

$$\text{Tense} \longrightarrow \begin{Bmatrix} \text{past} \\ \text{non-past} \end{Bmatrix}$$

What about the other meanings expressed by verbs which we have found – *perfect, progressive, habitual* and *stative*? Time reference is certainly involved, but it would be more accurate to describe them as having to do with perspective (e.g. 'current relevance') and with features or aspects of the action or event. Rather than including these quite different meanings under the category of tense, linguists have established another category, usually termed *aspect*. English shares this category of aspect with many other languages. For example, in Hindi[9] the affix *-taa* is added to a verb to show that the action is habitual, as in:

raam   rootii   Khaa- taa be
(Ram)   (bread) (eat- habitual) (English gloss)

English translation: Ram eats bread.

In this section we have described how linguists use formal analysis to set up grammatical categories such as tense, person, aspect, number, etc. Linguists start with the assumption that for each language there are a set of relevant grammatical categories. They use a range of techniques of formal analysis to identify these categories and describe completely and comprehensively how each language works. This description is part of a model or theory of the grammar of the language. In English there are formal differences in the verb, shown by various endings (*-ed, -ing, -s*) and by the co-occurrence with the main verb of the auxiliary verbs BE and HAVE. Their meanings and use are investigated, but, as we have seen here, correlations between the forms, the grammatical categories, and meanings are not necessarily one-to-one.

The negative in English

So far we have looked at three word classes in English and have seen how linguists operate at different levels in their analysis of how English grammar (or that of any language) works. We have seen how linguists observe variation in word forms and aspects of syntactic behaviour such as distribution, co-occurrence (what goes with what) and order – the position of a word in relation to other words in a sentence.

In some languages syntactic behaviour is largely a matter of variation in form. For example, in the Latin sentence, 'Marcus interfecit Sextum' (Marcus killed Sextus) the ending *-us* on the word *Marcus* tells us that he carried out the action of killing. This sentence can also be written or said in this way, 'Sextum interfecit Marcus' but it still has the same meaning – word order doesn't matter – the endings (inflections) give the listener or reader the necessary information to understand the sentence. However, in English, word order is very important to grammatical meaning. If we take the sentence, 'Hamlet killed Polonius' and change the order of the elements thus, 'Polonius killed Hamlet' the meaning is completely different. Instead of Hamlet doing the killing, now Polonius does.

In this section we will examine an area of English grammar which clearly demonstrates how central word order is – the area of negation.

English negative forms

Let's first look briefly at the negative forms in English. There are several. In the section on derivational morphology, we have mentioned the negative prefixes *dis-* and *un-*. There are also special negative forms which correspond to positive forms, e.g. *neither* and *nor* match with *either* and *or*. There are also single lexical items which have a negative meaning, for example *hardly*. 'I could hardly see a thing' is equivalent to 'I could see almost nothing'.

In this section, however, we will concentrate on the use of the negative word *not* in forming negative sentences. To make a sentence negative in English, we must insert the word *not* into the sentence. So negation in English is basically an insertion procedure. But the crucial question is *where* – what order of elements or words must a negative sentence have? We will start with a group of sentences and try to formulate as simple a rule as possible to account for the process of negation. Let's choose sentences with the verb *to be*:

Clare is happy.
The tea service was expensive.
He is here.
The book is on the desk.

The following are all ungrammatical:

*Not Clare is happy.
*The not tea service was expensive.
*He is here not.
*The book is on the not desk.

There is only one permissible position – after the verb.

We can formulate the following simple rule:

> TO MAKE A SENTENCE NEGATIVE:
> INSERT THE WORD 'NOT' AFTER THE VERB.

Now we will try this rule on another set of sentences:

> Jim hates beer.
> He left yesterday.
> We arrived on time.
> He read the book.

The result is unsatisfactory. If we follow the rule we get:

> *Jim hates not beer *He left not yesterday *He arrived not on time.

The correct forms are:

> Jim does not (or doesn't) hate beer.
> He did not (or didn't) leave yesterday.
> We did not arrive on time.
> He didn't read the book.

For this group of sentences, we need to insert the word *do* also. Our revised rule would be:

> TO MAKE A SENTENCE NEGATIVE:
> IF THE VERB IN THE SENTENCE IS 'TO BE', INSERT THE WORD 'NOT' AFTER THIS VERB.
> IF THE VERB IS NOT 'TO BE', INSERT THE APPROPRIATE FORM OF THE VERB 'DO' (*do/ does/ did*) AND THEN PLACE THE WORD 'NOT' AFTER IT.

(Notice that once *do* is inserted, that word now shows the tense in the sentence, (*did* for past, *do* for non-past) so the original verb returns to its basic form, e.g. *left* becomes *leave* in 'He left' – 'He didn't leave'.)

Now we expand the data again and check if we have a perfect rule yet. We will look at sentences in the perfect and progressive aspect:

> John has arrived.
> The book has been published.
> The children are singing.
> He is working hard.

These sentences complicate matters because they have more than one verb. Each has a verbal group with at least two verbs. Order is crucial here – we must specify that *not* is inserted after the first verb in the group, because we cannot have:

*John has arrived not.
*The book has been not published.
*He is working not hard.

We need a further modification to the rule we already have:

We now have a three-part rule which will transform all the following types of sentences into the negative:

The book is difficult. ⟶ The book is not difficult.

The book looks difficult. ⟶ The book doesn't look difficult.

The book has been made into a film. ⟶ The book hasn't been made into a film.

But what about the following sentence: 'The book which he wrote in two weeks became a best-seller.'? The problem we have here is that there are two verbal groups in the sentence – where do we insert *not*? Do we need to insert it twice? The sentence that we want is:

The book which he wrote in two weeks didn't become a bestseller.

The *main* idea is that the book did or did not become a best-seller. The part of the sentence 'which he wrote' simply gives us information about the book. But, unfortunately, our rule doesn't specify which verb to negate if there is more than one verbal group. We need to say that if there are two verbal groups in the sentence, the main verb is the one which has to be negated. Our rule has become more and more complicated. It must take account of the *total* structure of the sentence it applies to, including the status of the verbs; i.e. whether a verb is a main verb or simply a verb in a phrase which gives information about another part of the sentence (as in '. . . which he wrote . . .').

Summary of points

The area of negation illustrates how linguists proceed in their attempts to construct rules of grammar for a language. First, some data (sentences in the language) is selected, and as simple a rule as possible is devised to explain the data. Then the data base is expanded – more sentences are considered and the rule is checked for adequacy. If the new rule fails to account for the new data, it is revised. (Of course the revised rule must still account for the first set of data.) This process of expanding data and checking and reformulating continues until the linguist is satisfied that the final version accounts for all the data.

But modern linguistics involves more than discovering a set of grammar rules for a particular language. It is concerned with the general principles that underlie the particular rules of any language. The negation rule in English illustrates one of these principles – that the rules of grammar apply to structures of a general kind, not to specific words in specific sentences. The negative rule in English applies to the *verbal structure* of the sentence, and in sentences with more than one verbal group it must analyse the total structure of the sentences by recognising main and subordinate elements. In the next section we will explore this theme further.

Analysing sentence structure

The example of the rule for negative formation in English draws attention to another aspect of syntax which linguists must describe. Notice that we had to decide which verb to make negative, but that a rule which simply tells us to make the first verb negative is not satisfactory. We needed to examine the internal structure of the sentence. When we did this we discovered that the sentence 'The book which he wrote in two weeks became a best-seller' is very complex – it is really one sentence inside another. In other words, the sentence has two major parts or units. Each of these units has a structure closely resembling an independent sentence – they each have a verb and one or more nouns. One way to represent this fact is to put brackets around each of the units:

[the book [which he wrote in two weeks] became a best-seller]

To give more information about these two units we can label them. For example, we can use the label *clause* which simply means 'contains a verb', and identify Clause 1 and Clause 2. If we compare the following Sentence a) with other sentences, then differences or similarities in internal structure become clear:

a) The book which he wrote in two weeks became a best-seller.
b) I saw the man and he saw me.
c) The man who stole the money disappeared.
d) I saw the man.

Sentence a) is similar to b) and c) – they all have two clauses; and it is identical in structure to c) – they both have one clause inserted inside another. Sentence d) is quite different from a), b) and c) because it has only one clause.

But we can look at the internal structure of sentences in another way. We can also say that it is possible to divide Sentence a) into the following two units or components:

The book which he wrote in two weeks   became a best-seller

The justification for identifying these two components comes from a comparison with other sentences:

The awful book	became a best-seller.
Burmese Days	never became a best-seller.
The autobiography	might become a best-seller.
It	isn't worth reading.

What labels could we give these two components? Because a word from the class *noun* always occurs in the first part, and because it is very often a group of words (although it can contain just one word) we could call it a *noun phrase*. Since the other component always contains a verb, we can give it the label *verb phrase*. The following simple set of symbols represents this structure:

$$S \longrightarrow NP + VP$$

This is equivalent to saying: a sentence (S) consists of two parts, a noun phrase (NP) and a verb phrase (VP).

Of course there are some exceptional sentences in English which do not conform to this structure:

No entry.   Checkmate.   Good evening.   Hi!
Happy Birthday!   No kidding.   Really!
OK   The more, the merrier.   Full marks.

All of these are essentially formulaic expressions and are not counter-examples to the basic structure rule $S \longrightarrow NP + VP$. There are also cases where parts of the basic structure are omitted:

John: What are you doing?
Sue: Just thinking.

In her reply Sue has left out the words 'I am'. She has given an *elliptical* response – these are extremely common in conversations.

Let us examine the two major units NP and VP more closely. The examples above show that there are several possible types of NP. An NP can have a determiner (*the* or *a* or *this*, etc.); it can be a proper noun (e.g. *Burmese Days, John Winston*); it can be a pronoun; it can have an adjective (*old, awful*). We can write the following rule to indicate the possibilities:

$$NP \longrightarrow \begin{cases} det + N \\ proper\ noun \\ det + adj + N \\ pronoun \end{cases}$$

(the curly brackets indicate that the members of the list are options – any one can be chosen, but not more than one, or we could get '*it the long book', which is ungrammatical).

But how can we be sure that what we have identified is really a unit? What evidence can we use? There are several types of evidence:

a) the first evidence is substitutibility. We can substitute one type of NP for another, so if we have 'Mary lost her temper' we can substitute *she* for *Mary*. If we have 'the fascinating book' we can substitute *Burmese Days*. Substitutibility can be used as evidence of equivalence, or at least that two things belong to a particular group or class.

b) another type of evidence is that NPs resist being broken up and moved to other positions in the sentence. We cannot separate the determiner *the* and the adjective *fascinating* and move them to different positions. If we try, then the result is an ungrammatical sentence, e.g. *the became book a fascinating best seller.

c) the third type of evidence is the converse of b). It is possible to move NPs as a whole into different positions, for example, we can make five different sentences with the NP *the child*:

> The child ate the apple.
> The apple was eaten by the child.
> It was the child who ate the apple.
> What the child did was eat the apple.
> What happened was the child ate the apple.

d) a fourth criterion is that NPs have rules and operations that apply to them as *units*. For example, there are order constraints on the elements in the NP: – if we have one of the det + adj + N type, then these elements must occur in that order. We cannot have '*fascinating the book'. Another example is the operation of insertion involving NPs with adjectives. It is possible to insert or increase the number of adjectives as long as we do this between the determiner and the noun – 'the big green perfect apple'. In fact, technically there is no limit to how many adjectives can be included in any NP.

All these criteria can be used to demonstrate that the NP is a unit or *constituent* of sentences in English. This type of procedure in linguistics is termed 'Immediate Constituent Analysis' or 'Constituent Structure Analysis' and is the central notion in what is called 'Structural Linguistics'. One of the most influential linguists of this school was Leonard Bloomfield (1887–1949). His most important book was entitled *Language* and was published in 1933.

Note that if we want to be absolutely certain that we have identified a unit of structure, we would have to apply the same tests to other possible

Leonard Bloomfield (1887–1949) His influential book, Language, *established him as the foremost structural linguist of his generation.*

candidates as units. Let's try this by making an arbitrary cut at the fourth word of the sentence:

the book which he / wrote in two weeks became a best-seller

Can we find anything that we can substitute for this group of words? No. Can we change its position and create other grammatical sentences? No. Can we find any internal operations to carry out on it? Clearly not; 'the book which he' behaves like what it is – a mere sequence of words.

Once linguists have identified a constituent structure in one language, they speculate about whether it is relevant for other languages. So we can ask – do other languages have NPs? The answer seems to be yes, they do. It might even be the case that all languages have the constituent NP – if this proves to be the case, then we can say we have discovered a 'syntactic universal'.

Hierarchy

The analysis of sentences into constituents reveals that sentences do not have a simple linear organisation. Of course, in speech one word follows another in time, and on the page, one word follows another from left to right (or right to left, or top to bottom in languages other than English). But it is only on the surface that sentences seem to have a simple linear organisation. Our analysis of constituents shows that they have a *hierarchical* structure at a deeper level. If we want to represent the hierarchical structure of a sentence, we might draw it like this:

The cat saw the bird.

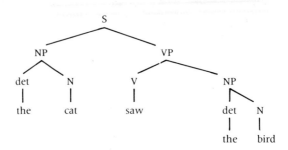

This diagram tells us that the sentence has two constituents, NP and VP. It also shows that the two NPs can be broken down themselves into two more constituents, e.g. *the* and *cat* are immediate constituents of NP. If you trace back in the diagram from N – (*cat*) the next constituent label you reach is NP. Similarly, if you trace back from NP, the next label you meet is S. So this diagram shows the constituent structure of the sentence and it shows that there is a hierarchy in the relationships between the constituents. The notion of hierarchy is very important in syntactic analysis.

Further analysis

Now that we have some new analytical tools – the notion of constituents and of hierarchical structure, we can return to our example sentence 'The book which he wrote in two weeks became a best-seller' and analyse it further. We have said that this sentence is really two sentences in one – that one sentence has been inserted inside another. But if we take into account our analysis of any English sentence into NP + VP then we can be even more accurate – we can say that a sentence has been inserted into the NP of another sentence:

the book *he wrote the book in two weeks* became a best-seller.
[s1   [s2   s2]   s1]

This means that we have another type of NP to add to our list of possible types of NPs: NP ⟶ (det) + N (+s).

The next task is to describe the steps involved in getting from the form above to the well-formed sentence 'The book which he wrote in two weeks became a best-seller'. (Remember that we are trying to represent what is going on in a hypothetical English speaker's mind as he or she is 'building' this sentence.)

For clarity we will label our two sentences S1 and S2 with S2 being the sentence which will be inserted (or to use the technical term *'embedded'*) in S1. We can represent S1 and S2 with the following diagrams (known as 'tree diagrams' – they have 'branches'):

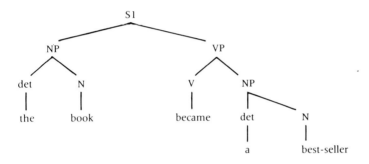

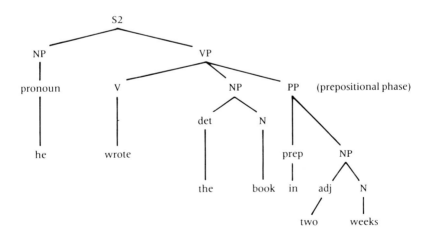

81

The next step is to embed S2 into the NP of S1. (So here we are using our rule N ———▶ (det) + N (+ s). We give a shortened version here:

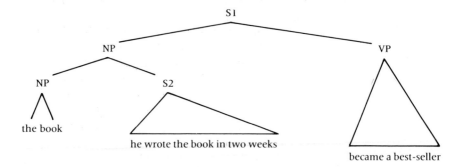

Now we must carry out specific changes:
1) we identify the NP in S2 which is identical to an NP in S1
   the book he wrote **the book** in two weeks became a best-seller
2) then we have to change the position of this identical NP; it must be moved to the front of its sentence. This gives the result: the book the book he wrote in two weeks became a best seller
3) then we delete the NP in S2 and replace it with a relative pronoun – we have two choices:
   a) *who* is used for animate nouns.
   b) *which* or *that* is used for inanimate nouns.

   Since *book* is inanimate, we can replace it with *which*. This step is known as *relativisation*.

Our final result is the perfect sentence:

   The book which he wrote in two weeks became a best-seller.

Using the symbols we have devised, this rule can be summarised and represented as follows:

   Relativisation rule:
   Structural Description: NP + s (x − NP − y)
   Structural Change: NP + s (rel pron − x − y)

   The structural description describes the type of sentence that a particular operation can be carried out on. Here it describes any sentence which has the structure of NP with a sentence 'inside it' which also has an NP. So this rule could not apply to the sentence 'I saw the man'. The structural change is the set of changes – changes of position, insertion, etc. that must be carried out to form a perfectly grammatical sentence.

X and Y represent other constituents in the sentences, but they don't have to be given labels in our rule because they do not affect the operation of the rule. Of course, we could include the labels if we wanted to.

We now have a rule which will describe all English sentences with this internal structure, and will predict the occurrence of all other such sentences. This type of rule is known as a *transformational rule* because it carries out radical restructuring of sentences. Such rules are central to the grammatical theory known as *Transformational–Generative Grammar*. This type of grammar is most closely associated with Noam Chomsky (1928–) and has, since the late 1950s, been very influential in linguistics. Its aim is to construct a theory of grammar which:

> would have very explicit rules specifying what combinations of basic elements would result in well-formed sentences . . .[10]

It sets out to construct rules which will generate all and only the well-formed sentences in a particular language. As we have pointed out

Noam Chomsky (1928–) He has been a major influence on linguistics since the 1950s, and is most closely associated with the theory of Transformational–Generative Grammar.

before, native speakers perform all these changes unconsciously as they build sentences in their heads, but a formal grammar of a language must reflect or 'capture' what native speakers know and do.

There are further modifications to sentences like this and because we want our set of rules to be complete, and to account for everything, we need to devise some extra parts to this rule. For example, it is possible to delete the relative pronoun and still have a perfectly grammatical sentence:

The book he wrote in two weeks became a best-seller.

This relative pronoun deletion is optional, so we must stipulate that our rule for this step is optional:

Relativisation rule 2 (optional):
Structural Description: NP + s (rel pro − x − y)
Structural Change: NP + s (x − y).

But we must proceed with care − we have a potential problem with this optional rule. If we have a sentence such as:

The man who is wearing a black leather jacket is a famous actor.

which has as its source the two sentences:

The man is wearing a black leather jacket.
The man is a famous actor.

we cannot delete the relative pronoun *who*. If we did, the result would be an ungrammatical sentence:

*The man is wearing a black leather jacket is a famous actor.

Why? What has gone wrong with our rule? If we compare the internal structure of the two sentences, we notice a difference: in our example sentence the identical NP which was relativised is the object of its verb:

He wrote what?   He wrote the book.

But in this sentence the identical NP is not the object of the sentence to be inserted, but the subject:

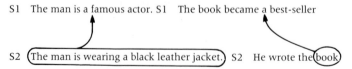

S1   The man is a famous actor. S1   The book became a best-seller

S2   The man is wearing a black leather jacket. S2   He wrote the book

So these sentences are not exactly alike in structure, and the difference is a crucial one when we carry out the relativisation rule. When the relativised NP is the subject of its source sentence, then *who* or *which* cannot be deleted. But when the relativised NP is the object of its source sentence, then the relative pronoun can be deleted.

By examining relativised sentences we have seen how rules that we formulate to account for these structures involve the following:

—insertion e.g. of the relative pronoun
—deletion   in some cases the relative pronoun can be deleted
—change in word order
—constituents must be recognised e.g. we had to find identical NPs

In the negative rule we also saw that bits were inserted (*not*); that word order was important (where to insert *not*); and that the rule applies to a particular constituent – the verb phrase. Let us now look at one more area to see how these procedures are carried out in the application of transformational rules.

The passive in English

In the previous sections we have seen how word order is important in English. Other languages make more use of inflections or special forms of words. The English sentence 1) 'Hamlet killed Polonius' means something completely different from 2) 'Polonius killed Hamlet'. Word order is used to show which person was the killer and which person died. We saw that in Latin different endings are added to the names to show who killed whom, so that word order does not matter. However, in English there is another way in which the meaning of 'Hamlet killed Polonius' can be conveyed:

3) Polonius was killed by Hamlet.

This form of the sentence has the same meaning as 'Hamlet killed Polonius' but word order and word forms are used together to show who killed whom. In traditional grammars of English 3) has been called a passive sentence, and 1) has been called the active version of that sentence. Native speakers know that 1) and 3) are related in a way that 1) and 2) are not, so linguists need to include rules which represent this knowledge. The following transformational rule has been proposed to account for the relationship between active and passive sentences:

Structural Description: NP1 + v + NP2
Structural Changes: NP2 + be + v –ed + by + NP1

The first part of the rule (the structural description) tells us that if we have a sentence with these constituents, then we can make a set of changes which will result in another sentence in English. Let us work through the changes:

First, the order of the two noun phrases must be changed – NP2 must be moved before the verb, and NP1 must be placed after the verb. At this stage we have:

NP2	V	NP1
Polonius	killed	Hamlet

Secondly, the word *by* must be inserted before NP1, so we get:

NP2	V		NP1
Polonius	killed	by	Hamlet

Thirdly, the form of the verb must be changed. A complex form with the auxiliary verb *to be* must be used – *killed* must be replaced by *was killed*. Notice that the tense after the structural changes are made must be the same as the tense before the structural changes were made – *killed* is past tense, so we need *was killed*, not *is killed* or *will be killed*. Our structural change says nothing about changing the tense of the verb, it only tells us to use a form with *to be*. We have now followed all of the instructions given in the structural changes and the result is:

NP2	TO BE	V		NP1
Polonius	was	killed	by	Hamlet.

which is a perfectly formed passive sentence. If we fail to apply any part of the rule then the result will be ungrammatical. For example, if we leave out the word *by* we would have: '*Polonius was killed Hamlet', a non-sentence.

Notice that both the active and passive sentences give us basically the same information about who is carrying out the action of *killing* and who is the (unfortunate) receiver of the action, but they use different syntactic signals to do this. This demonstrates how transformational rules can capture the fact that two sentences may be different in form but have the same meaning. In the active sentence, the word *Hamlet* has initial position in the sentence and it precedes a verb in a certain form. The word *Hamlet* has *subject* position – *Hamlet* is the doer of the action of killing. In the passive sentence, the word *Hamlet* is in final position in the sentence. It is preceded by a verb in a certain form – *was killed* – and by the word *by*. These two aspects of structure show again that the noun constituent *Hamlet* is the doer of the action of killing. Both sentences show, though with different means, that *Hamlet* has a certain relationship to the verb constituent *to kill* and that *Polonius* has a quite different relation to the constituent *to kill*. In the next section we will expand on this theme of the *relationships* between constituents.

Functional relations

In discussing two types of sentences – relativised sentences and passive sentences – we have mentioned how important the relations between constituents are. Let us look at other types of sentences where particular relations hold between constituents:

1) The petals of the blue poppy have fallen off.
2) That man's suit is poorly designed.
3) The poor people of Ethiopia have no homes.
4) The leader of the party gave a wonderful speech.

In Sentences 1 to 4 a special relation holds between the constituents of the first noun phrase – that of possession or belonging. In traditional grammar this is termed the *genitive*. In English there are two ways of marking the genitive – 1) the use of an apostrophe followed by the letter *s* (-*'s*) as in 'that man's suit', and 2) the use of the word *of* – as in 'the leader of the party'. The genitive in English is really a special kind of modifier – it specifies the noun more exactly. The word *man's* gives more information about the suit (who it belongs to) and *of the party* gives more information about the leader.

In English genitive constructions there are word order restrictions. For example, the word with the -*'s* must be positioned to the left of the noun it modifies: 'the suit man's' is ungrammatical. If an *of* construction is used, it must be positioned to the right of the noun – 'The of the party leader' is ungrammatical. The word order restrictions seem to apply generally to all modifiers in English: determiners such as *the*, *these*, *this* and adjectives (*big, little, beautiful*, etc.) must all precede the noun:

the tall man   this book   that table   the beautiful flower

Prepositional phrases generally follow the noun:

the hole in the wall   the house on the hill
the man in the room

In the case of the determiners *this/that, these/those* the restrictions on word order with respect to the noun are not the only restrictions that occur. The choice of *these* or *this* and *that* or *those* depends on the noun. If the noun is singular, then *this* or *that* must be used; if the noun is plural then the word *these* or *those* must be used. 'Those cat is purring' is ungrammatical, as is 'These apple is delicious'. The choice of *this/these* versus *that/those* also depends on the proximity of the objects to the speaker in space – if an object is relatively close to a speaker, *this* or *these* will be chosen; if it is relatively further away, *that* or *those* will be chosen. We can say that determiners must *agree* with the noun in number.

87

In earlier forms of English there was another type of agreement between nouns and other constituents. During the period which is known as Old English, roughly from 450 to 1150, there were different forms of *the* (the definite article). For example, the modern English phrases 'the good king', 'the good book' and 'the old ship', when translated into Old English would be:

se goda cyning   seo gode boc   þaet eald scip

Nouns in Old English were classified as masculine, feminine and neuter. With a masculine noun, the article *se* had to be used; *seo* was used with feminine nouns; and *þaet* was used with neuter nouns. (Notice the special letter at the beginning of *þaet* – this symbol has since disappeared from English spelling.) Masculine, feminine and neuter did not necessarily correspond to the biological sex of the noun – some nouns referring to females belonged to the neuter group, some nouns referring to males belonged to the feminine group, and objects, which of course have no biological sex, could belong to the masculine, feminine or neuter groups. Also notice the different forms of the word *good – gode* and *goda*. Again, in Old English, the choice of the form of the adjective depended on the class the noun belonged to – masculine, feminine, or neuter.

We can think of the noun in Old English as 'controlling' the other constituents of the noun phrase, and in Modern English this 'control' is shown through the positions of the other constituents – the determiners, adjectives, etc., and by agreement in number. As a general statement, we can say that the noun is the *head* of the noun phrase in which it occurs, and that the other constituents *depend* on the noun. The most basic evidence for this statement is that the noun is the only constituent which can occur alone – it is an obligatory constituent. There are some rare cases where we do have nounless noun phrases. An example is:

The rich get richer and the poor get poorer.

But when sentences like this are used, listeners interpret the adjective and determiner, e.g. *the rich*, as fulfilling the functions of the noun. In cases where there are two nouns in a noun phrase as in *bus station* and *computer software*, the listener or reader will interpret the rightmost noun as the head noun, and the noun to the left of it (*bus, computer*) will be interpreted as fulfilling the functions of a modifier.

The dependency relationship between head noun and modifiers even extends to meaning – the meaning of *tall* is quite different when it is modifying the noun *woman* and the noun *building*. This is generally true of all adjectives which refer to an extreme point on a scale e.g. *good – bad rough – smooth*.

It is important that any grammatical description of English makes clear the relationships between the head noun and its dependent determiners and modifiers. If we are using structure rules such as those which have been described in previous sections of this chapter, e.g. NP ➞ (det) + N, then we could stipulate that if there is an N on both sides of the arrow, then the N on the right-hand side is the *head* of the construction on the left-hand side:

$$NP \longrightarrow (det) + (adj) + N$$

We could also show the function of the head noun in another way – we might draw a tree diagram in which the *head* constituent is shown as having dependent modifiers:

So for the sentence 'The petals of the blue poppy have fallen off', part of the tree would look like this:

In languages such as Modern German and Old English, in which the determiners and modifiers must agree with the noun in gender, this type of diagram shows the way the gender of the noun 'spreads downward' to the other constituents. The gender of the noun is copied by the determiners and modifiers.

Following our analysis of the NP where one constituent is head and 'governs' other constituents in terms of form and meaning, can we extend this analysis to the sentence as a whole? Can we find one constituent of the *sentence* on which all the others depend? Some linguists have given a positive answer to this question. They have proposed that the verb of the sentence is the central element, and that all the other noun phrases, prepositional phrases, adverbs, etc., have particular relationships to the verb. Let's look at the way sentences can be analysed as a central verb, with other constituents which have a function or 'role' in relation to the verb. We shall go back to the Shakespearean example, and expand it a bit:

Hamlet killed Polonius with a sword.

We can say (as we have hinted already) that the relationship between Hamlet and the verb *kill* is that Hamlet is the *doer* of the action – or the *agent*. Polonius is the *object* or *patient* or *receiver* of the action. And, in our expanded version, the *sword* is the *instrument* or *tool*. These functional relationships are shown in a diagram like this:

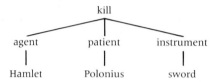

This is an alternative analysis of sentence structure to the ones we have exemplified so far using NP and VP constituents. The distinguishing feature of the type of diagram shown above is that *functional* information is explicitly included in the analysis in the form of labels such as *agent*, *patient* and *instrument*. Instead of using labels such as NP and VP which are constituent labels, we use *functional labels*.

Trying to incorporate functional relations into the analysis of sentences does not mean that there is no interest in syntactic categories such as NP and VP. It simply means that the analysis is saying that, at the most basic level, this type of functional information is important – that it is *primary*.

In this section we have seen how function is a key notion in grammar. In the next chapter we will take this further and explore the function of sentences in texts and conversations. But before we do that, we will look at some examples of 'grammar in action'.

Grammar in action

Pronouns in action

We have examined the pronoun system of English in relation to the categories: number, person and gender. In this section we will briefly examine some of the ways that English speakers exploit pronouns. As it is a *closed system* it would seem that speakers of English would be restricted or locked into a simple set of choices, but this is only true to a certain extent. However, when choices that seem to stretch the system to its limits are used, they are always meaningful – the speaker is doing it for some reason or effect. Look at the following:

1) She's a real beauty.
2) It is due in June.
3) She has great potential.

If the speakers of these three sentences are following the established conventions of pronoun reference in English then the *she* of 1) and 3) is a female animate being, perhaps an actress, a horse, a ballerina, etc. and the *it* of 2) is an inanimate object, perhaps a financial report, a dissertation, etc. But it is possible for *a real beauty* to be a plane or a ship or car. In the British Navy ships are often referred to as *she* and airline pilots or chauffeurs often refer to the vehicles they fly, drive, etc. as *she*.

What seems to be involved here is that a pronoun which is usually reserved for female animate beings is being used as a way of showing personal interest – a way of saying 'I have the same depth of feeling for this object as I would have for a fellow human being'.

Conversely, one would never expect an animate being to be referred to as *it*, but in 2) *it* could be an unborn child, which is expected in June. Clearly in this case, it is used because the sex of the child is not yet known. In the case of countries being referred to as *she*, which is a possible meaning in example 3), Jespersen[11] claims that there is a historical reason for this. In Latin and French, the names of countries were always feminine in gender, and English simply followed the pattern. *Nature* was also a feminine noun in French and Latin, and this may be the reason why English can have sentences such as: 'Nature is cruel; she has no pity'. In English poetry there are many examples of inanimate objects or abstract concepts being addressed or referred to as *she*:

> Let Fate reach me how she likes . . .
> Robert Browning[12]

This usage seems to be part of a Western literary tradition.

From these examples, we can say that a distinction between the animate and the inanimate is encoded into the pronoun system of English, but that speakers use the system in order to convey a range of attitudes towards objects, people and entities.

Exploiting 'we'

We have already discussed the use of inclusive or exclusive *we* in relation to speakers and hearers, but there is a variety of ways *we* can be used in English. Here is one example – a headmaster of a school is addressing the entire school in the morning assembly. Two of the pupils have been asked to stand up in front of all the others, because the headmaster knows they have been found stealing fruit from a garden near the school:

> We have to know who the thieves are so we can protect our belongings.[13]

Notice how the headmaster uses *we* to isolate the two boys. *We* includes himself, the teachers, the administrators, the other pupils, in fact, everyone he is addressing except the two boys. He sets up a distinction between the two boys and the rest of the school, identifies them as thieves, makes them outcasts. By doing this he hopes to make them feel ashamed and prevent them committing further misdeeds. This use of *we* is very powerful.

We can be used in a quite different way – to create a feeling of togetherness and solidarity. The leaders of nations, large organisations and political parties often use *we* to refer to the whole group and to indicate their role or position as spokesman/woman or leader. Here are some examples:

> We as a people will get to the Promised Land.
>
> (Martin Luther King)
>
> We will pay any price, bear any burden, meet any hardship, support any friend, oppose any foe, to assure the survival and success of liberty.
>
> (John F Kennedy)
>
> We must both defend freedom and preserve the peace.
>
> (Ronald Reagan)

As well as being used to build solidarity, this technique also underlines the separation between *we* and others (another political party, a nation, an enemy, etc.)

Sometimes *we* is used to show something about the relationship between speaker and addressee. Mothers often speak to their children using *we* instead of *you*:

> One more spoonful – we must finish our breakfast if we want to grow up big and strong.

Doctors and nurses occasionally use the pronoun with patients to achieve a coaxing, caring tone:

> How are we feeling today?

But some patients may feel that this insults their individuality and interpret it as condescending, perhaps because they associate it with the way mothers talk to their young children.

These examples show that the pronoun system is exploited in various ways by speakers, but, interestingly, English pronouns do not have meanings of formality and status and respect as do the pronoun systems of many other languages. For example, in German, the pronoun *Sie* is used to address elders, those with higher status, and strangers. *Du* is used for family and those with lower status. Perhaps the only pronoun use in

English that does signal status is that reserved for the monarch. The king or queen, when addressing the people of Britain, will use the 'royal' *we* instead of the pronoun *I*. Queen Victoria became famous for the phrase 'We are not amused'. Supposedly, she had a strict idea of what was and was not humorous and would use this expression to show her displeasure. (Some claim that this is actually not true.) When Margaret Thatcher's daughter-in-law had a child, Mrs Thatcher is reported as saying, 'We have become a grandmother'. She was vehemently attacked in some newspapers, and by the leader of the opposition party, Mr Kinnock, for seeming to give herself a special status reserved only for the Queen. Such is the power of pronoun use.

The passive in action

As a grammatical transformation, the passive rule gives the speaker or writer flexibility in arranging the order of elements, particularly noun phrases, in a sentence. But writers and speakers would not bother with re-arranging the order of constituents unless this had some meaning or effect, so what is the effect of putting an NP at the end of a sentence rather than at the beginning?

Two principles seem to be of importance: *end-weight* and *end-focus*. End-focus in sentences is similar to the idea of building to a climax in narratives and other longer stretches of speech. When telling a joke, one doesn't say the punch-line first, one builds up the suspense and expectations of the audience. Action-adventure stories, mysteries, thrillers, plays, rock performances, symphonies, all build towards a climax:

> Guess what? The marathon was won by a woman who had never run that distance before in her life!
> I don't believe it. The criminal was caught by a young child.

End-weight is the second guiding principle. 'Weight' in this sense is measured in syntactic terms: the longer a phrase or clause is, the weightier it is; and the more modifiers or subordinate clauses it has, the more weighty it is in terms of grammar. In the examples above, the phrase 'a woman who had never run that distance before in her life' is very 'heavy' and the phrase 'a young child' is quite 'light'.

The principles of end-weight and end-focus often work together, because very often the weightier a phrase is, the more information it has, so it is placed at the end of the sentence through the use of the passive transformation. These two principles are clearly working together in the first of the examples above. In the following text the phrase 'any fall of more than a few dozen feet' is placed at the end of the last sentence using the passive in line with these two principles.

For their surface area, insects weigh very little. A beetle, falling from a high altitude, quickly achieves terminal velocity: air resistance prevents it from falling very fast, and, after alighting on the ground, it will walk away, apparently none the worse for the experience. The same is true of small mammals – squirrels, say. A mouse can be dropped down a thousand-foot mine shaft and, if the ground is soft, will arrive dazed but essentially unhurt. In contrast, human beings are characteristically maimed or killed by *any fall of more than a few dozen feet.*[14]

This text also illustrates another way in which the passive can be exploited in English. It is possible to use an optional transformation to delete the agent, for example, 'I dropped the glass' ⟶ 'The glass was dropped by me' ⟶ 'The glass was dropped'. In the text, the sentence about the mouse has undergone agent deletion because who drops the mouse is unimportant and in a sense irrelevant to the meaning.

In the example, 'The plate was dropped by me' the agent is important, but note that it is possible for a speaker to conceal the agent by deleting it. The passive clearly has much to do with communicative effects and with the construction of texts.

The negative in action

We have looked at how negative sentences are formed in English and the way that an insertion-type rule can account for the native speaker's knowledge about forming negative sentences. But how do speakers exercise choice? How do they choose between negative and positive sentences? An obvious answer is that they choose negatives when they have something negative to say, but this simple answer needs closer investigation.

In many cases speakers actually have quite a few options:

Clare is happy.	Clare is not happy.
Clare is unhappy.	Clare is not unhappy.
John is awake.	John is asleep.
John is not awake.	John is not asleep.

The negative of the sentence 'John is awake' is 'John is not awake', but a speaker could also choose to say 'John is asleep' as *asleep* is synonymous with *not awake* (see section on sense relations in Chapter One). Is there any difference? There does seem to be. Very often, when a speaker uses a negative sentence it is because they are *denying* something. So if a speaker decides to say 'John is not awake' it may well be because someone else has just said 'John is awake' and the speaker wants to deny the truth of this statement (he or she has just seen John asleep).

This means that negative sentences require special attention from listeners, and listeners will tend to interpret them as a denial of a previous assertion in many cases. It is as if the listener is saying to him/herself – 'Why is the speaker using a negative sentence when a positive one could have been used? There must be a reason – it must be a denial'.

To support this argument two types of evidence can be presented. The first is that, in general, negatives are less informative than positive sentences. For example, of these three statements:

1) The Mona Lisa was painted by da Vinci.
2) The Mona Lisa was not painted by Michelangelo.
3) The Mona Lisa was not painted by Rembrandt.

all of which are true, 1) is the most informative, and the two negative sentences, 2) and 3), are the least. The number of people who did not paint the Mona Lisa is very large indeed; the number who did paint it is simply one – da Vinci.

Leech[15] calls this the 'principle of negative informativeness'. He says that the 'world's population of negative facts is far greater than its population of positive facts . . . and (therefore) a negative sentence will be avoided if a positive one can be used in its place . . .'[16] So a listener who overheard someone say 'The Mona Lisa was not painted by Rembrandt' would probably assume that someone else had just asserted that 'The Mona Lisa was painted by Rembrandt'.

The second piece of evidence comes from psycholinguistic research. Several experimental studies[17] have been carried out in which people had to judge the truth or falsity of sentences like:

a) Fifty-seven is not an even number.
b) Twenty-four is an odd number.
c) Twelve is not an odd number.

It was found that denials like a) and c) took people half a second longer to judge than positive sentences like b). It is likely that this is because to process a) and c) the listener needs first to formulate the positive version, for example 'fifty-seven is an even number' and decide whether it is true or false. It then takes additional processing time to realise that if the positive version is true, the denial of it must be false, or, as in our example, if the positive version is false (fifty-seven is an odd number, not an even one) then the denial of it is true. Negatives are thus 'harder' for listeners to process, and speakers do not use them without a good reason.

A president's blunder
In the example sentences about the painter of the Mona Lisa, we said

that it was likely that if someone overheard 'The Mona Lisa was not painted by Rembrandt' they would assume it was a denial of a previous spoken assertion. But there may be 'unspoken assertions', that is, assumptions. People may assume from, say, how others are behaving or reacting, that they hold certain assumptions. For example, imagine that a man who has lost his door key arrives home. He tries to open one of the windows of his house to get in. A woman passer-by sees him and stops, looking at him closely. On observing this he might say 'I am not a thief' and then explain his situation. The passer-by's assumption that he was a burglar was not spoken, but because of her behaviour, it was clearly part of the context of the situation. The man's denial was very revealing of his state of mind.

A particularly interesting example of this phenomenon is the reaction to a statement made by President Nixon during the 'Watergate Crisis' in the 1970s. The newspapers were full of reports and articles about the burglary at the Campaign Headquarters of the Democratic Party (Watergate) and the possibility that this burglary had been carried out with the President's knowledge and that Nixon was involved in a 'cover-up'. If it were proved that he was involved, then Nixon could have been impeached (removed from the office of President) by the Congress. The only way he could have avoided this was to resign before he was impeached. At a news conference, while he was still fighting for his political life, Nixon said 'I am not a crook'. Herbert Clark, a linguist at Stanford University, records his reaction when he heard this remark by the President:

> We all knew immediately that Nixon shouldn't have said what he said. He wanted to assure everyone that he was an honest man, but the wording he used was to deny that he was a crook. Why should he deny that? He must have believed that his audience was entertaining the possibility that he was a crook and he was trying to disabuse them of this belief. But in so doing, he was tacitly acknowledging that people were entertaining this possibility, and this was something that he had never acknowledged before in public. Here then was a public admission that he was in trouble, and this signalled a change in his public posture.[18]

Nixon resigned shortly after making this statement at the press conference.

The above is an excellent example of an issue that will be the focus of the next chapter. How do listeners build bridges in conversation and in reading texts? How do they draw inferences from what they hear? The complementary question is 'How do speakers cause listeners to draw the inferences they want them to?'. Nixon did not want his audience to infer that he was worried that people thought he was a crook – that is why his utterance can be seen as a blunder.

References
[1] R.H. Robins *A Short History of Linguistics* (Longman 1967) p.33
[2] H. Jackson *Words and Their Meaning* (Longman 1988) p.16
[3] L. Bloomfield *Language* (Holt Reinhardt and Winston 1933) p.257
[4] see Sweet's *Anglo-Saxon Reader* (revised by D. Whitelock) (Oxford University Press 1967)
[5] The determiners in English are: *the*; *a(n)*; *my*, *our*, etc; *some*; *any*; *no*; *enough*; *this/that*; *every*; *each*; *either/neither*; *these/those*; *much*.
[6] see R. Quirk and S. Greenbaum *The University Grammar of English*, Section Four, for further details and examples (Longman 1973)
[7] see E.K. Brown and J. Miller for a brief discussion of the history of 'levels' in linguistics *Syntax: A Linguistic Introduction to Sentence Structure* (Hutchinson 1980) p.244
[8] This data was presented by John Sinclair of the University of Birmingham, lecturing on the Collins Cobuild Project in Madrid in February 1988
[9] A. Saksens 'Verb Agreement in Hindi' *Linguistics* Vol. 19 5/6 1981
[10] G. Yule *The Study of Language* (Cambridge University Press 1985) p.81
[11] O. Jespersen *The Philosophy of Grammar* (George Allen and Unwin 1924) p.235
[12] cited in Jespersen (1924) p.236
[13] S. Eales 'Language and Control in the Classroom' (unpub. M. Ed diss. 1983) North East London Polytechnic
[14] text from C. Sagan *The Dragons of Eden* (Ballantine 1977) p.87
[15] G. Leech *The Principles of Pragmatics* (Longman 1983) p.101
[16] Leech (1983) p.100–101
[17] see for further details H. Clark and E. Clark *Psychology and Language* (Harcourt Brace Jovanovich 1977) pp.107–110
[18] H. Clark 'Inferences in Comprehension' in D. LaBerge and S.J. Samuels (Eds) *Basic Processes in Reading and Comprehension* (Lawrence Erlbaum Associates 1977) p.188

Chapter Four

Texts and conversations

Before we examine the way sentences are used in written texts we need to consider what a *text* is. One could simply say that a text is sentences in sequence, but we will see that this definition is not adequate.

What is a text?

Read the following two passages:

A)

Pick up a handful of soil in your garden. Ordinary, unexciting earth. Yet it is one of Nature's miracles, and one of her most complex products. Your success as a gardener will largely depend upon its condition, so take the first bold step in gardening – get to know your soil.

B)

Fertilizers put back what the rain and plants take away. Plastic pots are not just substitutes for clay ones. Pears are a little more temperamental than apples. Supporting and training are not quite the same thing.[1]

Passage A is clearly a text. You probably had little difficulty in understanding it, even if you are not interested in the topic, and you probably were able to guess that it might be an extract from a book on gardening or agriculture (which it is). But Passage B is quite different – it is 'non-text'. In fact, it was created by copying the first sentence from every fifth page in the book on gardening that Passage A comes from. You probably found yourself wondering what the passage was about, and might have thought that something was missing or mixed up. Each of the four sentences is a perfectly grammatical English sentence but together they do not form a *text*.

Text analysis

In text analysis one of the primary tasks is to explore the linguistic features which characterise *texts*. Texts have structure, just as single sentences have structure, but the structure of texts depends on features which are different from those we observed in Chapter Three when we examined the way linguists describe sentence structure. The goal of text analysis is to examine how the reader or user of a text recognises that the words/phrases/sentences in a text must be co-interpreted – that parts of texts are dependent on others. One of the most important features of texts is that they have *cohesion*. Readers recognise this cohesion. In reading Passages A and B a reader recognises that whereas Passage A has cohesion, Passage B does not – it does not 'hang together'.

Text cohesion

The elements of a text are 'tied together' – the phrase *cohesive ties* has been used to refer to the features of a text which show which words, phrases/sentences are relevant to which others. In the analysis of cohesion in English texts Halliday and Hasan's *Cohesion in English*[2] (1976) has made a central contribution. They categorised cohesive ties into two basic types: lexical and grammatical. The following text illustrates the different types of lexical cohesive ties:

> Until fairly recently, nearly all waterworks in both industrialised and developing countries were originally built with one particular objective in mind. It might have been hydroelectric power, irrigation, swamp drainage, or some other purpose. A secondary benefit, such as flood control in the case of a river in the Monsoon area, might have accrued when a large dam was built, but would not have been a primary consideration in the matter.[3]

The most straightforward lexical cohesive tie is the repetition of a word or phrase – an example is the word *built* in Sentence 1, repeated in Sentence 3. The use of synonyms also ties a text together: *objective* and *purpose* are synonyms. (Of course, the writer had a choice – he/she could have repeated the word *objective*.)

The lexical relationship of hyponymy may also aid cohesion. An example in the text is the pair *waterworks* and *dam* – *waterworks* is the more general term (the *superordinate* term – see Chapter One on *sense relations*). A dam is a kind of waterworks. This lexical relationship adds to the cohesion of the text. Another lexical device is the use of the general noun *matter* to replace the phrase *when a large dam was built* in the last sentence.

Words that collocate (see Chapter One) also function as the 'glue' which makes a text 'stick together' at the level of lexis. In the passage we have *industrialised* and *developing* – both of which collocate with *country*. *Flood*, *river* and *swamp* form a kind of 'chain' of lexical items which share collocational potential and therefore help to establish the context or subject matter of the text.

Grammatical cohesive devices

Halliday and Hasan identified four types of grammatical cohesion:

conjunction   substitution   ellipsis   co-reference

In text analysis, these have been compared to 'signposts' on a road or map reference points – they tell the reader '. . . where he is going in relation to where he has come from'.[4]

Conjunction

The following text[5] illustrates devices of *conjunction*:

It is generally agreed that the earth's capacity to provide resources and to absorb wastes must be finite. Furthermore, there is little argument but that the earth as a whole is over-populated. Hence, action is urgently needed. As to the precise nature of that action, however, and how it is to be arrived at, there is great disagreement. In short, it is a problem which at present has no obvious solution.

a) *Furthermore* is an example of an *additive* type of marker or link which signals an addition to a previous element. Other examples are:

and   also   moreover   that is   alternatively

b) *Hence* is an example of the *causal* type of link – the need for action is caused by the problems described in the first two sentences. Other examples are:

thus   consequently   therefore   it follows   for this reason

c) *However* signals a change of direction in the development of the text. It is an example of what Halliday and Hasan term *adversative* cohesive ties. (It might have also been positioned at the very beginning of the fourth sentence.) As soon as the reader sees this word he/she knows that the description of the situation (problems and action needed) has been completed, and a different topic or concern will follow. In this particular text, the change in direction involves the agreement about the situation versus the **dis**agreement about exactly what to do. Adversative markers are similar to the road signs which tell a driver that the next bit of the road is different from the previous bit – it is 'one way' or 'a dual carriageway' or has a particular speed limit or driving conditions:

Other adversative markers in English are:

yet   although   but   nevertheless   instead   on the contrary

Grammatical substitution and ellipsis

These two types of grammatical cohesion can be treated together. In English there are five items which commonly substitute for nouns (and noun phrases), verbs (and verb phrases) and clauses:

one(s)   the same   do/did   so   not

The following short text illustrates their use. The item is circled and an arrow points to the word, phrase or clause that it is replacing (under-lined).

> For centuries the wind has been harnessed for mechanical tasks, in particular for pumping water. Simple windmills were in fact so used in ancient Persia and China. In recent times more powerful ones have been used in Holland to make vast areas of land suitable for agriculture, by pumping away the sea water. The Dutch also developed saw-mills, corn-mills, oil-mills and paper-mills – all of which worked just as efficiently as windmills did. Following Holland's success, many countries did the same. Most met with great success; some not.[6]

Ellipsis is 'substitution by zero' – a bit of the structure of a sentence is omitted and can only be 'recovered' by the reader from the previous discourse. Here's an example:

> The top priority for some countries is to tackle unemployment, and for others inflation.
>
> the top priority is to tackle

Co-reference

The fourth type of grammatical cohesion is co-reference. (Halliday and Hasan use the term *reference* but since this term is commonly used in the discussion of word meaning (see Chapter One) we will use *co-reference*). This term also has the advantage of emphasising the fact that items in a text refer to each other.

In the following text notice how the pronouns are used to co-refer to *dam, Mozambique* and *1969*:

> In 1969 work began on the construction of a vast dam 1
> across the Zambesi River. When complete **it** will irrigate 2
> 1.6 million hectares of land. But since **then**, and 3
> particularly since **its** independence, Mozambique has 4
> become increasingly worried about the cost of completing 5
> and operating the project. Quite apart from **their** natural 6
> unease at the cost, fierce controversy has surrounded the 7
> project from **its** beginning. Many are worried about the 8
> environmental implications of the project.[7] 9

In order to discover what *it* in line 2 refers to, the reader must look back to the previous sentence. This has been termed *anaphoric* reference; in order to understand the word *its* in line 4 the reader must look forward (to *Mozambique*) – this is termed *cataphoric* reference. The word *then* can only be understood as referring to 1969. Deictic items such as *this, these, those* and words such as *such, likewise, same* are also used to tie a text together through co-reference, but by far the most common referential device is the use of pronouns – readers must be able to identify the persons or objects that pronouns such as *it, he, they, she* refer to in order to understand a text. If a reader of the above text thinks that the pronoun *it* in line 2 refers to the Zambesi River instead of the dam, then he or she has not understood the text.

A closer look at use of pronouns for reference

The above analysis of the role of pronouns as a cohesive tie seems to suggest that *whenever* a reader comes across a pronoun he/she must search backwards or forwards for the noun or noun phrase that it is substituting for – its *co-referent*. But we need to examine this rather simple view more closely. Sometimes the referent has not been mentioned explicitly, but has only been *implied*. Here is an example:

> I had been waiting at the bus stop for over twenty minutes. At last I saw the bus coming, but as I moved out to get on, he just kept going even though he obviously saw me. I was so angry.

There is no word or phrase that *he* can be said to *substitute* for. What the reader does is use the knowledge that a bus has a driver and that *he* must refer to the driver – unless the reader is living under some strange misconception that buses are male and can make decisions about whether to stop or not! Something similar happens when we read the text about the dam in Mozambique; we use our knowledge that a country has people to interpret the word *their* in line 6.

Pronouns are not simple substitutes as are the word *did* and *so* discussed above. It is not the case that the reader works backwards to an 'original' noun or noun phrase or forwards to an anticipated noun or noun phrase. Imagine someone tells you a story about a man beginning in the following way:

I met a real idiot the other day who . . .

As the story progresses the man is referred to with many other noun phrases such as *this guy, the fool* and of course the pronoun *he*. By the end of the story you probably won't even remember the original phrase used at the beginning of the story, and if you were reading the story you wouldn't look back to earlier parts of the text each time you saw the word *he*. Rather, you would build a 'mental representation' of the person and relate each *he* or other expression to your mental representation.

This argument may seem obvious, but in a text that involves an object or objects that undergo changes then it is clear that pronouns cannot be seen as simply substitutions for the 'original' noun or noun phrase. The following recipe is an example:

Buttered Apples

One of the nicest and simplest ways of serving apples. Put the sliced and peeled apples into a fireproof dish. For 1lb of apples put 1 ounce of butter cut in pieces on the top, two tablespoons of brown sugar, and a piece of lemon peel. Put the dish uncovered, and without any water into the top of a medium oven, for about 30 minutes. Have a look at them from time to time and turn them so that all get equally cooked. They are nice hot or cold.[8]

In this recipe the apples referred to by the pronouns *them* and *they* are not the same apples in the first line of the recipe. A change of state has been brought about by the addition of other ingredients and by the heat of the oven. If we substitute the word *apples* from the first line (since it is the original referring expression) for the word *they* in the last line ('Apples are nice hot or cold'), and we interpret this as a general statement about this type of fruit, then it is clear that we have not understood the text as the writer intended.

So far we have been looking at illustrations of cohesion in quite short texts. Let's now analyse a much longer text of five paragraphs; this text was written by Ingmar Bergman, the famous film director.

> People ask me what are my intentions with my films – my aims. It is a difficult and dangerous question, and I usually give an evasive answer: I try to tell the truth about the human condition, the truth as I see it. This answer seems to satisfy everyone, but it is not quite correct. I prefer to describe what I would like my aim to be.
>
> There is an old story of how the cathedral of Chartres was struck by lightning and burned to the ground. Then thousands of people came from all points of the compass, like a giant procession of ants, and together they began to rebuild the cathedral on its old site. They worked until the building was completed – master builders, artists, labourers, clowns, noblemen, priests, burghers. But they all remained anonymous, and no one knows to this day who built the cathedral of Chartres.
>
> Regardless of my own beliefs and my own doubts, which are unimportant in this connection, it is my opinion that art lost its basic creative drive the moment it was separated from worship. It severed an umbilical cord and now lives its own sterile life, generating and degenerating itself. In former days the artist remained unknown and his work was to the glory of God. He lived and died without being more or less important than other artisans; 'eternal values', 'immortality' and 'masterpiece' were terms not applicable in this case. The ability to create was a gift. In such a world flourished invulnerable assurance and natural humility.
>
> Today the individual has become the highest form and the greatest bane of artistic creation. The smallest wound or plaint of the ego is examined under a microscope as if it were of eternal importance. The artist considers his isolation, his subjectivity, his individualism almost holy. Thus we finally gather in one large pen, where we stand and bleat about our loneliness without listening to each other and without realising that we are smothering each other to death. The individualists stare into each other's eyes and yet deny the existence of each other.
>
> Thus if I am asked what I would like the general purpose of my films to be, I would reply that I want to be one of the artists who built the cathedral on the great plain. I want to make a dragon's head, an angel, a devil, or perhaps a saint out of stone. It does not matter which; it is the sense of satisfaction that counts. Regardless of whether I believe or not, whether I am a Christian or not, I would play my part in the collective building of the cathedral.[9]

We can summarise the cohesive ties in the first paragraph diagramma-
tically as follows:

    ask—question—answer—tell   intentions— aims
    question—it   answer—it   the truth—the truth as I see it
    truth—it   my—I—I—I—I

We can find similar devices in the second paragraph, but there doesn't
seem to be any cohesion between the second and the first paragraphs –
not even a single lexical link or repetition. However, the reader expects
that the second paragraph is linked to the first. Why? One reason is that
the paragraphs follow on from each other – they are presented as a long
text and to a certain extent the reader assumes that they do make up a
text. (When you read the example of the non-text at the beginning of this
chapter, you probably made the same assumption – it was printed on the
page as a continuous text, so you automatically assumed that it was one.)
Also, the reader realises that the text is somewhat strange if the second
and following paragraphs do *not* have something to do with the first. The
sense of strangeness and even incompleteness would come from the fact
that there is a question in the first paragraph – what are his intentions
with his films? – which the director is going to answer, explaining exactly
what he means. A brief answer is given in the final sentence of the first
paragraph, but the reader probably expects that further comment will
follow. Even though this further comment is not to be found in Paragraph
2, which seems to be a little story about the building of Chartres
Cathedral, the reader assumes that the example of Chartres is somehow
linked to the full answer about the aims of making films.

But this further comment is also not found in Paragraph 3, although
there is some cohesion between Paragraphs 2 and 3. *Art, the artist, artisans,
worship* form lexical links, and *in former days* obviously refers to the past
times including the period when Chartres was built, burned and rebuilt –
the *old story*. (Notice that there is a link between *in former days* and the use
of past tense for past time in Paragraph 2.)

Paragraph 4 still does not provide the reader with the full answer about
the director's intentions in making films, but there are clear links with
Paragraph 3 – if Paragraph 3 is about a particular interpretation of the
artist, then Paragraph 4 describes a contrasting interpretation – one that is
held *today*. There are also some lexical links: *in former times – today, art –
artistic creation, the artist*, etc.

Paragraph Five begins with the word *Thus* which is obviously being
used by the writer to signal that what is to follow is a consequence of all
the points that have been made before. The film director aligns himself
with the artists he has described in Paragraphs 2 and 3, and against the

individualistic view put forward in Paragraph 4. The reader now finds some logical links with Paragraph 2 – the little story about the builders of Chartres – the film director wants to be like the people who built the Cathedral at Chartres.

What is interesting about this text is that there are relatively few cohesive links, especially in certain parts of the text e.g. between Paragraphs 1 and 2, but even without these explicit links the text has coherence and readers assume that the writer is 'going somewhere'. The cohesive devices in a language do not *make* a particular text hang together – they do not make it *coherent*. The coherence of a text exists at a much deeper level. We can say that there are underlying semantic relations that have the cohesive power. An interesting way to demonstrate this is to go back to the text about the problems of the earth and remove all the sentence-initial cohesive links. Only a few lexical and grammatical links are left but the text still has *coherence*:

> It is generally agreed that the earth's capacity to provide resources and to absorb wastes must be finite. There is little argument but that the earth as a whole is over-populated. Action is urgently needed. As to the precise nature of that action, and how it is to be arrived at, there is great disagreement. It is a problem which at present has no obvious solution.

One important explanation for why this short text still works as a text instead of becoming less coherent and cohesive is that it follows a very typical pattern or structure for texts – the *problem/solution* pattern. Readers can easily recognise this pattern – and other types of patterns – and are able to use their familiarity with the pattern to understand the text. In text analysis this notion of general patterns is very important. Let us examine this pattern in more detail.

The 'problem-solution' text structure

This text pattern or *macrostructure* has been described as having the following elements:

Situation or problem
Solution or response
Result or evaluation

Here is an extremely simple example of a text with this structure:

> I was on guard duty. I saw the enemy approaching. I opened fire. I beat off the attack.[10]

If the last sentence is omitted, the reader will feel that 'something is missing' – the success or failure of the response (opening fire) to the problem (the enemy attack) has not been mentioned. The problem is left unsolved and the feeling is that the text is 'to be continued'.

An experiment carried out with texts about traffic problems showed how sensitive readers are to the problem-solution macrostructure.[11] Two long texts were chosen, and four different summaries were written. One of the summaries was a 'good' summary which included all parts of the macrostructure; the second summary distorted the original text because it left out any mention of the problem; the third summary left out any mention of the solution; the fourth was a random summary, written by summarising every third sentence of the original texts.

All the subjects in the experiment were asked to read the original texts and the sets of four summaries, and then rank the summaries in order of preference. All subjects, with the exception of one, chose the 'good' summary as the best of the four, and the 'random' summary as the worst. These results provide firm evidence of the 'reality' of the problem-solution macrostructure. Even more interesting is the fact that some of the speakers in this experiment were non-native speakers of English – so perhaps this shows that some macrostructures are universal to all languages.

Another type of evidence about the validity of the problem-solution structure is that we find it in such a wide variety of texts. Edward Lear was a Victorian artist, who also enjoyed writing short humorous verses to entertain the young children he knew. Some of these 'limericks'[12] demonstrate the problem-solution structure.

> There was a Young Lady whose nose,
> Was so long that it reached to her toes;
> So she hired an Old Lady, whose conduct was steady,
> To carry that wonderful nose.

> There was an Old Person of Mold,
> Who shrank from sensations of cold;
> So he purchased some muffs, some furs and some fluffs,
> And wrapped himself up from the cold.

> There was an old person of Dutton,
> Whose head was so small as a button:
> So to make it look big, he purchased a wig,
> And rapidly rushed around Dutton.

Let us examine a longer example of the problem-solution macrostructure. This text is about the number of wild anmimals killed on the roads:[13]

Situation
or
Problem

Millions of animals, from badgers, hedgehogs, foxes and stoats to frogs and toads, are killed on Britain's roads each year. One estimate for US roads puts the carnage there at over a million wild animals killed each day.

And it isn't only the animals that are in danger. Hitting a full grown badger weighing 15 kilograms – or a deer weighing far more – at speed on the road, or trying to take avoiding action, can put people's lives at risk too.

Solution
or
Response

Reflectors are a simple and effective means of deterring deer. Fixed to posts at 15 metre intervals along both roadsides, they reflect car headlights off the road and into the roadside habitat, giving deer advance warning of a car's approach.

Result
or
Evaluation

West German reflector trials have achieved up to 40% fewer deer accidents. Trials are under way in the UK to see if they will deter badgers when they're fixed to shorter posts. In the Netherlands – where they are also being tested with hares – and Sweden, reflectors appear to be successful in keeping badgers at bay.

But reflectors have their problems. Vandalism is one. They also need regular cleaning to keep them shining and vegetation has to be controlled to stop it obscuring them.

Until all us motorists get it into our heads that we have not God-given, sole right of use of our roads – and that we could drive with a little more care – reflectors, and other techniques such as fences, marked animal crossings, sound-scarers, etc., are all there is to cut down on the carnage.

We have looked in detail at one particular macrostructure – the problem-solution structure. But there are other types of structure as well. The text by the film director has the overall pattern of question-answer. This is also a very common macrostructure. These patterns are one of the features that characterise *texts* as opposed to *non-texts* and they are very important in the process of comprehension. In the next section we will examine how *background knowledge* contributes to the comprehension of texts.

Background knowledge

What we understand of something depends on what we know about it – our past experiences and learning. This has been termed *background knowledge*. In our minds we have stored away all sorts of information, and it is stored in an organised way. This organised knowledge is used in the process of understanding texts. Read the following short texts and notice how certain background knowledge you have about 1) telephoning 2) watching a film 3) travelling by air 4) eating in a restaurant is activated.

> This is an answering machine. When you hear the tone, leave your message.
> We went to the cinema, but there were no tickets left. So we booked for the next matinee.
> Your attention please. Lufthansa announces the departure of Flight 675 to New York.
> 'Would you like to order now?' she said. 'Yes, I'll have the chicken.'

So, our background knowledge is organised and can be activated as needed to understand texts. We can talk in terms of *expectations*. For example, if you go into a take-away restaurant, you know that you go to a particular place to give your order, pay, and then receive your food wrapped up in some way – in a bag or box. (If it were to be given to you on a plate your expectations would not be fulfilled!) In fact, the experience of being in an unfamiliar situation is an unsettling one for people, and they often express their anxiety by saying 'I don't know what to *expect*'.

Our knowledge of the world is organised into *schemata, frames, scenarios* (many different terms have been used) and we can access these areas of knowledge to help us understand written texts. The four examples above are all examples of schemata or scenarios – the 'eating in a restaurant scenario', 'travelling by air scenario', etc. The process of understanding a text is thus an interactive one – the reader's background knowledge interacts with the words and structures of the text. Moreover, it is these *schemata* or *mental models* which enable readers to solve ambiguities or select between alternative interpretations in a text. So we can even say that the text itself is really only a guide to the writer's intended meaning, which the reader in a sense *re-constructs*. Reading a text is not a simple passive process, but a very active one.

Some researchers have used the term *scripts* to refer to the sets of expectations readers bring to a text. A script has been defined as 'the set of stereotypic expectations about the content in a given text'.[14] These expectations can even enable readers to complete unfinished texts with great ease. For example, what word(s) would you put in the blank below?

> Jim had an accident the other day; he cut himself with a
> _____.

Scripts or *schemata* also enable people to draw inferences from texts. For example, one script people might have stored in their minds is 'attending a conference'. This includes knowing about registration tables, name tags, the fact that there are shared social activities such as meals, a programme detailing lectures, and that people interested in the same topic will be there, that some of them will probably have met before, etc. So if someone who has been to a conference writes you a letter and says 'I wasn't even given a name tag or a programme' you are able to interpret that remark – to draw the inference that the conference was not well-organised – because the information about having a name tag to ease identification and a programme to inform people of the timetable of events is part of your script or schemata for conferences.

Researchers have found various types of experimental evidence for schemata. In some studies, people have been given a label for a particular schemata or scenario such as 'visiting the doctor' and asked to make up lists of expected events. Their lists are extremely similar to each other. When these events are put in a random order and other subjects are asked to put them in sequence, their responses are again very similar. If people are given a title or label that activates a particular scenario and are then asked to make up questions about the content of a text with that title, they come up with very similar questions. For example, the following titles all activate the scenario 'changing power':

A Military Takeover in (country name)
Corporate President retires
Resignation of President _____
Inauguration of Premier _____

If people are asked to make a list of the questions that they would expect to get answers for if reading a text with any of these titles, they include questions like the following:
   – Who is the new leader?
   – How did he or she come to power?
   – Was the change of power anticipated?
   – What is the reaction of others to this change?
   – What is known about the new leader?
   – What problems will he or she be facing?[15]

Background knowledge plays a very important role in the understanding or *processing* of texts. Research in text analysis has identified two types of *processing* – *bottom-up processing* and *top-down processing. Bottom-up processing* involves working out the meaning of words and the syntactic relations between words to build up a composite meaning. But at the same time people use other types of information – their stored knowledge of the world – to make predictions about what will probably come next in the text, or to decide what the meaning of some ambiguous part of the text is. They use top-down processing.

Summary

In this section we have explored the notion of structure in texts and looked at the way people make sense of texts. In the next sections we will look at how linguists have explored the structure of 'spoken texts' – the analysis of conversation.

Conversation analysis

In the previous section we were concerned with how linguists have studied written texts – text analysis – but this study forms only a part of the interest in linguistics about how sentences are combined in sequence to produce cohesive and coherent stretches of language. In recent years there has been an increasing interest in studying the structure of stretches of spoken language. *Discourse analysis* is concerned with studying how people use language in a variety of *discourses* – conversation, interviews, spoken commentaries, political speeches, teaching, etc. The analysis of spoken language involves the investigation of what people are trying to accomplish with their words and with the overall patterns that can be found in conversation. As in text analysis, the speakers' beliefs and expectations, their knowledge of the world, and the social conventions that exist in particular cultures about **how** to construct a message are of central importance. In fact, the terms *discourse* and *text* have been used interchangeably in linguistics. Some linguists talk about 'spoken and written texts'; some about 'spoken and written discourse'.

We have seen how writers make choices in the creation of written texts – they have a range of devices to exploit (e.g. cohesive devices) and a range of text structures – *macrostructures* to expound. In the creation of spoken texts – whether spontaneous, as in ordinary conversation, or pre-planned, as in a public speech, speakers also have choices about how to convey their meaning and intentions – how to accomplish their goals. In theory, anyone can say anything, but in practice, speakers are constrained by social convention. So in a sense we can say that there are 'rules' for speaking just as there are rules of grammar in a language. The study of these rules, and of the factors that govern choice by language-users in social interaction, has been called *pragmatics*. A central part of the field of pragmatics is the theory of *speech acts*.

The theory of speech acts

We commonly think of speaking to each other as a process of exchanging information:

A: What's your name?
B: Kenneth Miles.

111

But besides exchanging information, people do many other things when they speak. Let's begin by looking at a conversation between two people. The setting is the office of a private detective. The speakers are the detective, Sam Marlowe and his secretary Ella Perine. A potential client (a woman) has come into the outer office, presented her card, and asked to see the detective. The secretary has gone into the detective's private office and told him that someone wants to see him and given him the card.

Sam Marlowe:	(reading the card)
	Brenda Salford. Is that Miss
	or Mrs, Ella?
Ella Perine:	Mrs Salford, and her eyes are
	as cold as ice.
Sam Marlowe:	In other words, you don't like
	her?
Ella Perine:	I didn't say that.
Sam Marlowe:	But you don't?

What is each of the participants doing in this short conversation? There *is* an exchange of information, but when the secretary gives her boss the information about Mrs Salford's eyes, she is doing more than describing a physical feature. 'Cold eyes' is a metaphor for cruelty and lack of scruples, so with this remark the secretary is performing an action – she is *warning* her boss to be careful in his dealings with this client. At this point in the conversation the detective might even have said 'Thanks, I'll keep that in mind' to show his gratitude for the warning. But he seems to want more information about why his secretary has made this statement about the potential client. So he constructs an interpretation of what she has said based on his background knowledge that describing someone as having cold eyes is not a compliment. He hypothesises that she has said this because she dislikes the woman or has formed a negative impression of her from the way she looks or speaks. He then asks her to confirm whether or not his interpretation is correct – his remark is a *request for confirmation.*

The secretary now responds to this *act.* Her reply is not straightforward – instead of simply agreeing with the interpretation ('No, I don't'), she tries to avoid this by *asserting* that she did not say the words 'I don't like her'. But the detective is persistent – he knows that people don't always say exactly what they mean and that they often prefer not to express strong feelings of dislike for someone (another part of his knowledge of the world) so he repeats his request for confirmation: 'But you don't?'.

In order to make sense of what is happening in this short conversation, we must talk in terms of the actions the people perform with their words

– they warn, formulate interpretations and ask for confirmation, make assertions, etc.

'Speech acts'

The British philosopher, J.L. Austin, was the first to draw attention to the actions performed by speakers in *How to do things with words* published in 1962.[16] Austin's work was based on the observation that, while some utterances[17] can be used and are used to give information and report states of affairs, there are other utterances which must be treated as the performance of an act. Imagine that the detective's secretary walked into his office the next day and said 'I have found a better job. I resign'. In saying the words 'I resign' she has performed an action. Austin called this utterance a *performative*. Here are some other examples:

> I promise to do my best.
> I nominate John Fletcher.
> I bet you £10 that Mats Wilander wins.
> I sentence you to five years in prison.

Each of these utterances counts as an action. Notice that all are in the present tense. If someone says 'I promised to pay you five pounds' then they are reporting a past promise, not making a new one. Also it is not possible to say of any of these utterances that they are true or false. Another clue to the nature of these utterances is that *hereby* can be inserted after *I* – this calls attention to the fact that *by these means*, i.e. the uttering of words, an act is performed. Once we begin to analyse utterances from the perspective of what the speakers are doing, then it is possible to see that every utterance has some functional value. Even to say 'My name is _____' or 'It is half past twelve' is an act of *asserting*.

Linguists have identified many different speech acts. There are even speech acts which are tied to particular areas of social life. 'I sentence you . . .' and 'I fine you . . .' belong to legal situations, and there are utterances in sports and games which count as actions. For example:

> Fault! (in tennis the linesman declares that a service did not conform to the rules)
> Check! (in chess, one player attacks the other's king by saying this as he/she makes a move)
> Out! (in baseball, the umpire declares that a player has missed all his opportunities to hit the ball)

The complete set of speech acts has not been established (and in fact there may never be total agreement on what constitutes the complete set of speech acts). But there has been a lot of discussion about the basic *types* of

113

speech acts. J.R. Searle[18] has set up a classification of speech acts using five categories:

representatives   The speaker is committed in various ways to the truth of a statement.
Examples: believe, conclude, deny.

directives   The speaker is trying to get the hearer to do something.
Examples: command, insist, challenge.

commissives   The speaker is committed, in various degrees, to an action.
Examples: promise, guarantee, swear.

expressives   The speaker expresses an attitude about the situation.
Examples: deplore, congratulate, welcome.

declarations   The speaker alters a situation by making an utterance.
Examples: I resign, I declare war.

"I hereby pronounce you authorized personnel."

Conditions for 'success'

In order to be valid or successful, the performance of a speech act must satisfy certain conditions. For example, if another player – not the umpire – calls 'Out!' during a game of baseball, or if a spectator calls out 'Fault!' during a tennis match, then the conditions for the performance of these acts have not been fulfilled because the speakers did not have the authority to perform the act. With this point in mind let us reconsider the first dialogue used in this section where one person asks another his name.

A: What's your name?
B: Who wants to know?

It is clear that B is unwilling to give the information until he knows who is asking the question, and can then decide whether that person has a right to ask such a question. If a stranger walked up to you in the street and asked your name you would probably respond in the same way – or you might even say 'None of your business!'. If, however, we consider the setting of a military prison during wartime – the questioner is the commanding officer and the person being questioned is a captured soldier – then it is clear that the soldier would have to respond. Under the Geneva Convention on the treatment of prisoners of war an officer has the right to ask a captured soldier his name and the soldier has the obligation to respond.

J.R. Searle (1932–   ) of the University of California. His book, Speech Acts, *is a key one in the philosophical view of linguistics.*

115

This particular condition – the right to perform an act – is not relevant in the case of some speech acts, such as *betting* or *promising*. It is nonsensical to say that someone doesn't have the *right* to promise, thank, bet, etc., but there are other pre-conditions which must hold for certain speech acts to be valid. Take the case of commands. A pre-condition for commands is that the addressee has the ability to perform the action:

A: Open the door, please.
B: I can't – my hands are full.

If B thinks that A can clearly see that he is unable to perform the action, then he might get very irritated and reply:

B: Don't be so unreasonable! Can't you see my hands are full?

Another pre-condition for the performance of commands is that there is a reason to do the action:

A: Turn down that radio.
B: Why?

If A were a parent and B a child, A's reply might well be 'Because I say so!' – rights and reasons are very clear-cut in this situation.

Notice that an analysis of spoken language using these notions of speech acts and pre-conditions enables us to account for the coherence of conversation. We recognise that the following dialogue is not simply the unrelated utterances of two people – one describing a sound and the other describing a state of affairs (although it is of course conceivable that this is the case):

Jim: The doorbell is ringing.
Marie: I'm on the telephone.

Instead, we link the two utterances and assume that Jim is directing Marie to perform some action (see who is at the door) and Marie is refusing to do so because she is unable to. The coherence of this short spoken text derives from the relationship between two acts – the act of commanding and the act of refusing to obey. We could expand the dialogue to show this more clearly:

Jim: The doorbell is ringing – go and see who is there, Marie.
Marie: I can't, I'm on the telephone.

Notice that Marie doesn't give a simple refusal, but one that includes the information that she is unable to perform the action – she refers to the pre-condition of ability. Hers is an indirect refusal.

Indirect speech acts

Many speech acts are performed indirectly as in the above example. One might expect that people would normally ask a question by using an *interrogative* – a form beginning with *what/why/who/where*, etc. or an inverted question-form, e.g. 'Is she here?' or a form with *do, did, does*, etc. Likewise, the most direct way to give a command is to use the imperative sentence structure – 'Stop that!', 'Go away!', 'Come here!'. In making assertions one would be expected to use the declarative form, with subject-verb word order, e.g. 'The soup is too hot'.

But this is not always the case. In fact, very often people seem to prefer not to be direct and explicit in the performance of speech acts. In order to explore why this is so, we need to take account of the social relationships between speakers and hearers. Let's take the example of commands.

The complexities of commanding

Imagine you want someone to give you a match. If you were speaking to a very good friend then you might use a direct command in the imperative form 'Give me a match'. Because you know the other person very well it would be appropriate to be direct, although you would probably add the word *please* as a marker of politeness. But a master speaking to a servant, a commanding officer to a soldier, a boss to an employee, might also use the imperative form (and even omit the word *please*). In cases where participants have very different social status, then the person with the higher status has the right to order or command. But how would the person with low status behave if he/she needed a match? Most probably, markers of deference would be used, such as 'Would you give me a match, please?' (this is termed an embedded imperative). But what if you were speaking to a stranger? It might not be possible for you to tell whether the other person has higher or lower status than you, so you might choose to be indirect – instead of using the imperative form you might construct a question which relates to one of the pre-conditions for commands – e.g. whether the person has the ability to perform the action. So you might say: 'Have you got a match?'. You might be even more indirect by not addressing your question to an individual, but by asking a question about the 'surroundings': 'Is there a match around here somewhere?'. This would show that, if there were, you yourself would be willing to get it. Perhaps the most indirect approach you could take would be to make an assertion about your need for a match: 'I've forgotten my matches'.

So how people choose to perform acts in conversations depends on social factors such as status or role, or social position of the participants, and the social conventions that hold in particular societies. The conventions outlined above are not universal, but specific to British and to some extent American society. In another society, it might be conventional social behaviour to be direct when speaking to a stranger, or indirect and very polite when speaking to a subordinate.

If there are so many factors at work – social conventions, pre-conditions, preference for indirectness, etc., then how do listeners know how another person is using a particular utterance? Is what is heard a promise, a warning, an assertion, or . . . ? If you overheard the remark 'I'll pay you back', you would need a great deal of information in order to tell whether the speaker was threatening revenge, promising to pay a debt, or making an offer. First of all, you would need to know the context of the utterance – who is speaking to whom, what is their relationship, where they are, what has gone before, etc. But you would also be able to exploit your knowledge about the patterns and regularities of conversation – the structure of conversation – to arrive at an interpretation.

The structure of conversation

Linguists working in the field of conversational analysis have disco-vered patterns and regularities in the structure of conversations. A key observation is that participants take turns in conversation. This has led to the identification of rules for sequences in conversation.

For example, if a speaker A asks another speaker B a question, then the normal response of Speaker B is an answer. Or if Speaker A calls out B's name – to get his or her attention (a *summons*), then B's next utterance will probably count as an *answer* or *response to the summons*:

> *Mary:* John! There's a phone call for you.
> *John:* I'll be there in a minute.

Regular two-turn units such as these have been termed *adjacency pairs*. Some other examples are:

greeting—return of greeting	A:	Hello!
	B:	Oh, hello, what a surprise to see you!
thanks—acknowledgement	A:	Thank you so much!
	B:	Not at all – my pleasure.
apology—acceptance	A:	I'm really sorry.
	B:	That's OK – I understand.

In some cases there may be two options for the second speaker after the first part of the adjacency pair: if someone makes you an offer, then you may either accept or refuse. Or if someone complains, then the addressee can either express sympathy:

A: I'll never get all this work done on time – it's too much for one person.

B: You poor thing, it's not fair at all to ask you to do it all alone.

or diminish the complaint:

A: This is awful – I have to rewrite my assignment – the teacher says she can't read my writing.

B: Well, I'm not surprised, you really should have tried to be neater.

Of course it is possible for a speaker to delay the completion of an adjacency pair, and this is quite common in conversation:

A: Do you want an ice cream?

B: Do they have chocolate?

A: No, just vanilla and strawberry.

B: No thanks.

Speaker B obviously will only have an ice cream if chocolate is available, so he delays his answer until he has enough information to make a decision. A realises what is happening, and doesn't say 'I just asked you a question, why don't you answer?'. To do so would be to miss the fact that B is not simply answering a question by asking another, but engaging in a *side sequence* that is relevant to the initial question.

Speakers know about the rules and patterns of conversation and they rely on their expectations that, for example, what follows a question should be treated as an answer or as an utterance related to the act of *answering*, in order to help them interpret the function of utterances in a conversation – to help them 'read the other person's mind'.

Where there are patterns and regularities there can always be the possibility of broken patterns and irregularities. If a speaker does not take the expected turn after another person has spoken then this choice is seen as meaningful, not simply as a lapse. Imagine this conversation between two friends – they are sitting in the same room and both are reading. Jane looks up towards John and says his name to attract his attention – she has something she wants to discuss (she performs a *summons*):

Jane: John, listen to this – there's something really interesting in the newspaper.

On being summoned, John does not look up or say 'What?' or 'Yeah?' – he just keeps reading. After a few seconds, Jane says 'Are you mad at me?'.

Here, Jane has interpreted John's silence after having been summoned as a sign that he is angry with her and is showing his anger by refusing to have a conversation with her. His silence is full of meaning. In not responding, John is actually communicating something. And Jane's ability to interpret John's silence is an example of how people rely on their knowledge of how conversational interaction works – how it is organised. This knowledge goes far beyond knowing how to put words together in sequence to make grammatically well-formed sentences. And it also involves an understanding of meaning that is different from knowing the meaning of words (lexical meaning) and the meaning of syntactic structures (grammatical meaning). It involves knowing about the meaning of utterances in context – pragmatic meaning.

Of course people do 'get things wrong' – they do misinterpret the intended meaning of others. The following encounter is definitely odd:

A: (a stranger, map in hand, standing on a busy city street, stops a passer-by)
Excuse me, do you know the way to the bus station?
B: Yes, I do. (walks on without stopping)

The poor lost stranger was making a request for directions, not quizzing the local people on their knowledge of the city!

Sometimes people purposely misinterpret a speaker's intention for special effect. Here is an example:

(Two friends are sitting having a drink in a café)
A: How do you drink that awful beer?
B: I simply put the glass to my lips, take a sip and swallow.
A: Yes, yes – OK I won't say another word.

B has correctly interpreted A's utterance as a criticism of the quality of the beer he likes to drink and perhaps therefore of his own taste in beverages, and has decided the best way to counter the criticism is to pretend the remark was literally a request for information. A's reply (Yes, yes – OK) shows that he has understood that what B was really saying was something like 'Aren't you being impolite and impertinent by criticising my choice of drink?'. A 'answers' this question by agreeing with the criticism. Unless we propose an interpretation like this, then A's use of the word *yes* doesn't seem at all coherent. By pretending to interpret A's first utterance as a simple information question rather than the indirect criticism that it really is, B has managed to make a strong statement about A's right to criticise him in the first place.

Conversational principles

We have looked at the way speakers create coherent spoken texts by understanding the underlying functions of talk and the overall patterns of talk. But the successful conduct of conversation depends on the fact that speakers follow some extremely basic principles for conversing. These principles all focus on their shared view that conversation is by its nature cooperative. People follow *cooperative principles* in conversation, which affect such matters as the quality and quantity of speech – in other words, the truthfulness and informativeness of what is said.

Let us consider quality or truthfulness first. Speakers should not say what they believe to be false. We all know that people do lie, but we must proceed on the assumption that we are not being lied to. This basic assumption has been formulated as a *maxim* by H.P. Grice (1975):

> Maxim of Quality: Be truthful in conversation: do not say anything you believe to be false; do not say anything for which you lack adequate evidence.[19]

Of course, this principle applies to other types of social interaction besides conversation. We expect people we are working together with on some task to make genuine contributions. Take the example of two people washing dishes together – one is doing the washing and the other is handing him dishes to wash. The washer does not expect to be handed clean dishes to wash. Handing someone a clean dish to wash is really equivalent to a lie!

The second important principle in social interaction centres on the notion of quantity. To take a very simple example, if you go to a friend's house, and your host asks if you would like some tea, you do not expect, a few minutes later, to be handed two cups of tea at once. Or, to give another example, if A and B are working together to repair a car, and A needs a wrench, B does not expect B to hand her/him three wrenches. We expect people's contributions to be appropriate in quantity. In conversation this means that we expect what speakers say not to be too brief or full or overlong or overexplicit – but 'just enough'. We expect them to follow the principle of quantity or informativeness:

> Maximum of Quantity: Be as informative as is required, but not more informative than is required.

Here is an example[20] of a speaker who is not following the principle of quantity:

> (Two people are talking about a mutual friend who is male, married, and who enjoys eating out in restaurants)
>
> A: Jim is taking a woman out for dinner tonight to that new restaurant on Croom Street.
> B: Is his wife going too?
> A: Of course, the woman he is taking out is his wife.

In using the phrase *a woman* instead of the more informative phrase *his wife*, Speaker A was not following the Maxim of Quantity. Speaker B, however, assumed that he was and immediately asked a question based on the assumption that the woman was somebody other than Jim's wife, and because a husband might usually be expected to take his wife out to dinner most, if not all, of the time (note the reliance on background cultural knowledge) Speaker B wants to know whether Jim's wife is going too. What will B say next? It is very easy to guess – probably something like 'Why didn't you tell me he was taking his wife out in the first place?'.

Besides the two principles of quality and quantity, speakers also must be relevant and clear:

> Maxim of Relation: Make your contribution relevant to the aims of the conversation.
> Maxim of Manner: Be clear. Try to avoid obscurity, ambiguity, etc. in your use of language.

Listeners will assume that a speaker will follow these principles in any conversation, no matter how trivial, and if it seems to a listener that they are *not* being followed, the listener will interpret this as significant and try to figure out why the speaker is behaving in this way. Just as we saw that the failure to complete the first part of an adjacency pair is significant (silence or refusal to speak is meaningful), so failure to comply with these basic principles of conversation is also meaningful. Here is an example where B's utterance doesn't seem to be relevant or clear and A arrives at an explanation for this behaviour:

> A: Where's my new tennis racket?
> B: Lots of people suffer from tennis elbow if they play too often – it's a painful condition and sometimes you have to have injections, and it's very hot today – much too hot to play tennis, but it's a nice day for a walk in the park – why don't we go for a walk?
> A: You've borrowed my tennis racket and broken or lost it, haven't you?
> B: (with a guilty look) Yes, I'm sorry – I'll buy you another one.

The four principles of quality, quantity, relevance and clarity are essential if conversations are to be cooperative. But speakers may sometimes have extremely good reasons to break the basic parts of the cooperative principle. Let us consider an example:[21]

> (A group of friends are discussing the fact that Susan and Max, a couple they all know, are emigrating from Britain to Australia)

> *Ann:* I'll miss Susan and Max very much, won't you, Steve?
> *Steve:* Well, I'll miss Max.

On the surface, Steve seems to be breaking the Maxim of Quantity. He has only responded partially to Ann's question. Recognising this, Ann and the other listeners will draw the conclusion that Steve won't miss Susan because he doesn't like her. If they all draw this conclusion we might ask why Steve didn't simply say directly: 'I'll miss Max but not Susan because I don't like her'. The reason has to do with another principle which applies to conversation in addition to the cooperative principle – the *politeness* principle. Briefly, this principle requires speakers to 'minimise the expression of impolite beliefs'.[22] Steve could have been more informative, but only by being more impolite and expressing dislike for a fellow human being.

In British culture, the politeness principle probably accounts for the use of 'white lies' in conversation. For example, if someone invites another person to a party and that person wants to decline the invitation, rather than saying 'No, I don't want to come' the person might pretend to have another engagement and say 'Thank you, but I'm going out that evening'. Of course, after repeated invitations which are repeatedly declined with statements like 'I'm afraid I'm busy' or 'I have another engagement', the inviter will probably 'get the message' and stop the invitations.

White lies must of course be properly deceptive. Imagine someone who declined an invitation for dinner the following weekend by saying 'I think I'm going to have a headache'. In its transparency this 'white lie' is a failure – it breaks the politeness principle – and is perhaps even more impolite than a simple direct refusal.

Very often a superficial view is taken of politeness in spoken language – it is associated with being superficially 'nice', and with formal, mechanical extras such as the words *please* and *thank you* and the use of special constructions such as *would you mind . . .* or *could you . . .* or *I wonder if you could . . . .* But politeness is an all-pervasive principle and also involves the content of conversation, as we have seen in the above examples.

Another manifestation of the politeness principle is the *Maxim of Agreement*. In conversation, people tend to try to agree with those they are speaking with if at all possible – even to the extent that they exaggerate the degree to which they agree or even try to hide their underlying disagreement. In the following example, notice how much effort Speaker B puts into trying to hide the fact that Speaker A thinks one thing (the female being discussed is 'small') and he thinks the opposite.

> A: She's small, isn't she?
> B: Well, she's sort of small . . . certainly not very large . . . but

actually ... I would have to say that she is large rather than small.[23]

The above conversation is very different indeed from the following simple expression of disagreement:

A: She's small, isn't she?
B: No, she's large.

If expressing disagreement is inevitable, then speakers attempt to soften it in various ways, by expressing regret at the disagreement ('I'm sorry, but I can't agree with you'). Notice in this example the use of the word *can't*. This seems to imply that the speaker would like to agree. Speakers may even show reluctance to speak at all when they know they will be disagreeing – they use expressions such as *well* at the beginning of their utterances or they 'hum and haw'. Speakers also may express partial agreement if they can:

A: The film was very well-directed.
B: Yes, on the whole, although there were a few poor sequences, don't you think?

An interesting area of investigation is the study of different cultures and languages in relation to the social principles of conversing. For example, some cultures may place a very high value on the Maxim of Agreement and speakers may show this by repeating every word the other speaker has just said – as if they agree totally – and then giving their own opinion. The British are supposedly well-known for the use of 'yes, but . . .' replies. There is much interesting and important research to be done in this area of cultural norms. Let's look at one example – how people respond to compliments in British, Australian and American culture.

Compliment responses

A compliment requires a response, that is, it is another example of an adjacency pair. The simplest response an English speaker can make to a compliment is *thank you*. This is because a compliment is in a way a kind of gift, and conventionally you thank someone for giving you something. But although speakers do respond with a simple *thank you*, there seem to be other more common and perhaps, therefore, more preferred responses. In her investigation of compliment responses, Pomerantz[24] found that there seem to be two social principles behind these preferred responses: the first that it is preferable to agree with anything a speaker says to you (the Maxim of Agreement) rather than to reject it or disagree. The second is that a speaker should avoid or minimise self-praise in conversation. We can call this the 'Maxim of Self-praise Avoidance'.

But if someone gives you a compliment there is an unavoidable conflict between these two principles: if you agree with the compliment, this amounts to praising yourself. If someone says to you, 'You look wonderful' and you accept the compliment, then in a way, you are indirectly saying 'I look wonderful'.

But the adjacency pair must be completed – a response must be made, so what do English speakers do? Here are some examples from the world of sport.[25] In the televising of sports events, it is very common that the winner(s) and loser(s) are interviewed by a television reporter after the award, medal or trophy has been presented. When interviewing the winner(s) the sports reporter often starts out with a compliment. How does the winner respond?

> *Interviewer:* The New South Wales Open Champion – Martina Navra-
> tilova!
> How do you feel after playing so well?
> MN: Erm . . . well first I guess bad luck Hana . . . we had
> another tough match.

Winners often make an appeal to luck as the determining factor in their victory, as Martina Navratilova has done above. This is one strategy that can be used to avoid self-praise. By shifting the reason for the victory from the sports person's own excellence and talent to the notion of their 'good fortune' or the 'bad luck' of the opponent, he/she avoids saying 'I am the best – I am wonderful'. (Of course some sports personalities have become famous for not avoiding self-praise.)

Another strategy of self-praise avoidance is to shift the praise to another person. In the case of team sports, this may be another member of the team; in individual sports, credit may be shifted to a trainer, coach, etc. (and when that person is interviewed and praised, he or she will most likely shift the praise back to the sports person).

> *Interviewer:* You really looked as though you enjoyed this series . . .
> RN: Well . . . you know I have had a lot of help and a tip
> Glenn Turner gave me early on has been very beneficial.

The winner may also downgrade the significance of the victory by recalling a prior defeat, or poor performance. Another downgrading strategy is to say the winning performance was no different from normal performance ('I just went out and performed as if it were no special occasion').

Sometimes the interviewer does not only give a compliment but gives a summary of the victory which itself makes reference to 'luck' or how close the victory was – how the other side 'almost won'. If this happens then the interviewee need only agree in order to avoid self-praise. In a sense the television reporter has resolved the conflict between the Maxims of Agreement and Self-praise Avoidance for the sports person. Here is an example of how the sports commentator 'makes responding easier' for the winner by not giving a simple direct compliment:

> *Interviewer:* You must be delighted . . . ten wins in a row . . . but it
> was a very close race at times, wasn't it?
> SL: It was a very very hard fought race.

Note, however, how the winner intensifies the assessment – *very close race* is turned into *very very hard fought race.*

These examples come from the fairly informal situation of television sports interviews. The same patterns are also found in much more formal award ceremonies. The Nobel Prize ceremony is an example. In accepting their Nobel Prize, winners never express disagreement with the public evaluation of their achievements, but they very often reassign credit to colleagues, fellow researchers, other scientists, or authors, etc. They also often downgrade their achievements in order to avoid excessive self-praise.

Thus we see that there are clear parallels in compliment responses in many different contexts, both formal and informal. Such evidence supports the universality of the social principles of linguistic behaviour.

In this chapter we have been concerned with how utterances have meanings in situations – with how speakers create spoken texts in order to achieve specific goals and with how listeners manage to read the intentions of speakers. In a sense, communication can be seen as a kind of problem-solving. Both speaker and hearer are engaged in this problem-solving, but in slightly different ways. The speaker has a particular goal –a desired result – so the speaker must decide what the best way is to accomplish this goal. The hearer has a different kind of problem to solve; it could be formulated as follows: 'Given that someone has just said X to me, what did that person mean me to understand by that?'.[26]

Linguists who study pragmatics are interested in the way speakers and hearers solve the problem of communication. Because its main concern is with the meaning of utterances in social situations (using 'social' in its broadest sense) pragmatics needs to investigate the social principles behind the use of language. There are many constraints on speakers and hearers – 'freedom of speech' is a well-known expression referring to an abstract principle of human rights, but it rarely exists in its absolute literal sense in communication. There exists in every society a notion of what 'good communicative behaviour' is and the conventions about this behaviour must be followed by language users.

More language in action

The focus of this entire chapter has been on 'language in action'. We have looked at several examples of people acting through language; some of them have been hypothetical examples, some of them have been real. But, to round off the discussion, let us examine a few more real examples of people using language to accomplish goals. We include these examples to make it clear that, more often than not, people have several very complex goals in speaking, which they must accomplish simultaneously. The examples used in this chapter so far have perhaps given the impression that a single utterance has a single goal or responds to one particular principle of conversation – that speakers have a straightforward and simple set of choices to make. This is certainly not the case, and when we ask the question 'What was Speaker X doing with that utterance – what did Speaker X mean by that?', the answer to that question is very often extremely complex.

'Considering I am a hostage . . .'

The first example we examine is quoted by Leech.[27] It was said by a speaker in a very dangerous situation. He was one of the American hostages being held in Iran in 1980. His captors had announced that they were planning to release him. A press conference was arranged and he was allowed to answer questions posed by the world's press. Not surprisingly, at the press conference one of the reporters asked him how he was being treated. This was a difficult question to answer. If he replied 'I have been treated badly' then this might have angered his captors and they might have changed their minds about releasing him. It would also have upset his family, who he knew would be listening anxiously to the press conference, as well as the other concerned United States citizens listening to the news from Iran. He didn't want to affect these people in this way – he wanted to do just the opposite – to reassure them. But of course, he had to follow the Maxim of Quality – he couldn't say something that was obviously false – this in itself would have caused his listeners to read into his lie interpretations such as: 'They have told him what to say' or 'His captors are allowing this interview in order to present themselves as good, kind, just people – it is all a "set-up"'.

This is what he said in answer to the question 'Are you being treated badly?':

Considering I am a hostage, I am being treated fairly.

Notice that first of all he avoided saying his treatment was 'good' or 'bad' – he chose instead to shift his answer onto another aspect of treatment – whether it is 'fair' or 'unfair'. In doing this, he was still following the Maxim of Relevance because he was saying something about his treatment, but he restricted his answer to a different classification of treatment, whether it is fair or not. Someone can be treated badly, e.g. punished, but it may still be fair treatment if they themselves have done something to warrant the treatment.

Note also that if we think in terms of connotations, 'fair treatment' has very positive connotations. Rather than angering his captors by this phrase, he may even have pleased them by saying something which seems to indicate that they have a high moral sense. He also probably managed not to upset his family and friends by allowing them to interpret 'fair treatment' as possibly also being 'good' treatment.

His decision to respond by beginning 'Considering I am a hostage. . .' is also quite significant. He avoids making a statement about his treatment in universal or general terms – 'good' or 'bad' in *any* situation or context, and restricts his description to a much narrower context. There exists a range of treatment for people who are hostages – one expects physical restriction: certainly one doesn't expect to be allowed freedom of movement, and one doesn't expect to be in luxurious surroundings (although some hostages may be kept in plush surroundings). Within that narrow range of possible treatments he chooses to respond by categorising his treatment at the 'plus good' end of the scale. Of course this may not have been true, but it is believable to his listeners in a way that 'I am being treated well' is probably not believable.

Thus, in responding this way, in one short utterance, the speaker accomplished a variety of communication goals for a variety of listeners.

'Did you like her?'

This very simple question comes from a famous murder trial at the turn of the century – the Seddon case.[28] Seddon was accused of the murder of Miss Barrow, an old woman who lived in his house as his lodger. Miss Barrow had been his lodger for about a year, and it was known that she had some savings – not a lot of money, but she was by no means poor. When she died Seddon arranged for the funeral since Miss Barrow had no living relatives. Seddon arranged for her to be buried in a pauper's grave. This aroused suspicion because it was clear that if Miss Barrow had some money then that money could be used to arrange a respectable burial and to pay for a gravestone. It was considered to be a terrible thing to be buried in a pauper's grave, that is, in the cheapest possible coffin, with no gravestone to mark the grave, with the costs paid for by the church parish as an act of charity for the poor and destitute. Seddon was suspected of murdering Miss Barrow and stealing her money.

At the trial the prosecuting attorney had to prove Seddon guilty of murder – but to do this it was necessary to establish a motive. When he went into the witness box, Seddon denied the charge of murder, and the defending attorney emphasised the fact that there was no evidence that murder had been committed. The prosecuting attorney started the cross-examination with a very simple information question: 'Miss Barrow lived with you from July 26, 1910 to September 14, 1911?'. Seddon replied 'Yes, she did.' Then the attorney asked his second question: 'Did you like her?'. This very simple question devastated Seddon – he became confused and didn't seem able to reply. He knew he was trapped. If he said 'No, I didn't like her' then he knew he was revealing a motive for murder. But if he said 'Yes, I did' then he knew exactly what the attorney's next question would be – 'Why did you arrange to have her buried in a pauper's grave if you liked her?'. Eventually Seddon broke down under cross-examination and confessed to having murdered Miss Barrow and stolen her money.

The prosecuting attorney devised his question knowing how each answer would be interpreted by the jury. In courtroom questioning lawyers ask questions not because they do not know the answers, but because they are trying to establish a particular view of events through the questions and the answers. Their aim is to get from the witnesses a certain set of facts and then to rely on the background knowledge of the members of the jury and their ability to infer from a set of facts that certain events did or did not take place. Lawyers in a criminal trial never ask the defendant, 'Did you commit the crime?'. The defendant will of course deny committing the crime even if he/she did. Lawyers use the technique of questioning to control the perception and interpretation of a set of agreed facts – their use of language is persuasive.

Concluding remarks

In order to understand the nature of language, linguists start from the basis that they must take account of the fact that language 1) is a formal system and 2) has a social function.

In approaching language as a formal system, linguists examine language data, and try to discover the underlying patterns and regularities that make up the system. This is the *formalist* perspective on language. Any formal grammatical theory, for example, tries to represent what native speakers 'know' about their language. This knowledge about a language crucially involves knowing what is and what is not well-formed. For example, speakers of English know something is odd about the following:

> grass green on apple onceness
> The octopus flapped its wings.

In Chapter Two we examined the sound system of English as an example of the study of phonology – what sounds are used and how they are organised as a system. In Chapters One and Three we looked at words and sentences to discover how linguists go about trying to describe meaning and structure at these two levels of analysis. In linguistics, the aim is to develop a theory which accounts for the way speakers construct, create and use their language. These theories are usually formulated in terms of rules.

In Chapter Four we saw that a theory of pragmatics tries to represent what native speakers know about the use of language in communication – its social function. Pragmatics uses as its data the discourses that speakers construct. To account for what speakers and listeners do, pragmatics also tries to formulate rules – examples are the four maxims of the *Cooperative Principle*, the *Agreement Rule*, the *Self-praise Avoidance Rule*, etc.

But these rules are in a way different from the rules of the sound system or of morphology or syntax. If someone asks the question: 'Where do you come from?' and the addressee responds with:

> from I comed placeness in out twslip

then he/she has broken rules of English grammar, morphology and phonology – in a sense the answerer has said something which is not English. But if the addressee replies:

> I come from the planet Earth

then no rules of English have been broken, but he/she is not following the basic principle of *quantity* – the answer is not informative enough. (We must assume a normal context here – one person is speaking to another at a social gathering with the intent of starting a simple pleasant conversation with a stranger, and there is no question of anyone (or anything) other than earth dwellers being there.) So, rules about the use of language which relate to its social functions are more like guidelines, rather than strict rules. In studying language as it is used by speakers to accomplish communication goals, linguists take a *functionalist* perspective.

Throughout this survey of modern linguistics, three words have been used very frequently: *form, meaning* and *function*. In a sense these three words represent the major concerns of linguistics – the forms of language, the meaning of these forms and how they are used – their function in human communication.

References

[1] passages from Dr D.G. Hessayon *The Garden Expert* (Hazell Watson and Viney Ltd 1986)

[2] M.A.K. Halliday and R. Hasan *Cohesion in English* (Longman 1976)

[3] this example text comes from R. Williams 'Teaching the Recognition of Cohesive Ties in Reading in a Foreign Language' *Reading in a Foreign Language* Vol. 1 No. 1 1983

[4] R. Williams p.47

[5] Williams p.47

[6] Williams p.43

[7] adapted from Williams p.41

[8] E. David *French Country Cooking* (Penguin 1959) p.173

[9] this text and analysis after M. Hoey *On the Surface of Discourse* (Allen and Unwin 1983)

[10] R.M. Stanley 'The Recognition of Macrostructure: a pilot study' *Reading in a Foreign Language* Vol. 2 No.1 p.157

[11] R.M. Stanley p.160

[12] limericks from *The Complete Nonsense of Edward Lear* Holbrook Jackson (ed.) (Faber and Faber Ltd. 1947)

[13] this text is a shortened and adapted version of an article in The *Weekend Guardian* March 25–26, 1989

[14] J. Zuck and L. Zuck 'Scripts: an example from newspaper texts' *Reading in a Foreign Language* Vol. 2 No. 1 1984

[15] Zuck and Zuck p.148

[16] J. Austin *How to Do Things with Words* (Clarendon Press 1962)

[17] the term *utterance* will be used in reference to stretches of spoken language as opposed to written language, where *sentence* is used

[18] adapted by D. Crystal *Cambridge Encyclopedia of Language* (Cambridge University Press 1987)

[19] after H.P. Grice 'Logic and Conversation' in P. Cole and J.L. Morgan (eds.) *Speech Acts* (Academic Press 1975) p.41–58

[20] after H. Clark and E. Clark *Psychology and Language* (Harcourt Brace Jovanovich 1977)

[21] after G. Leech *Principles of Pragmatics* (Longman 1983)

[22] Leech p.81

[23] adapted from P. Brown and S. Levinson 'Universals in Language Usage: Politeness Phenomena' in E. Goody (ed.) *Questions and Politeness* (Cambridge University Press 1978)

24 A. Pomerantz 'Compliment Responses – notes on the cooperation of multiple constraints' in J. Schenkein (ed.) *Studies in the Organisation of Conversational Interaction* (Academic Press 1978)

25 examples adapted from M. Emmison 'Victors and Vanquished: the social organisation of congratulations and commiserations' *Language and Communication* Vol. 7 No.2 1987

26 see G. Leech (1983) section 2.5 on 'Pragmatics as Problem-solving' for further discussion

27 Leech (1983) p.23

28 this case is described in Sir D. Napley *The Technique of Persuasion* (Sweet and Maxwell 1975)